PILLARS OF OUR FAITH

Practical applications of prophecy and our fundamental beliefs

BRIAN D. JONES

Pacific Press® Publishing Association
Nampa, Idaho
Oshawa, Ontario, Canada

Edited by David C. Jarnes
Designed by Tim Larson
Cover illustration by Justinen Creative Group ©

Unless otherwise indicated, all Scripture quotations are from the New King James Version.

Library of Congress Cataloging-in-Publication Data

Jones, Brian, 1948-
Pillars of our faith / Brian D. Jones.
p. cm.
ISBN 0-8163-1833-6
1. Seventh-day Adventists—Doctrines. 2. Bible—Prophecies—End of the world. I. Title

BX6154 .J667 2001
230'.6732—dc21 00-68150

01 02 03 04 05 • 5 4 3 2 1

CONTENTS

INTRODUCTION

A young Irishman was the sole survivor of a shipwreck that occurred about a mile off the coast of Wales. He found a craggy rock jutting out of the sea and took refuge there, gazing hopefully toward the shore and the cluster of sympathetic onlookers who had gathered. But the waters were too treacherous to attempt a rescue then. All night the young man—cold, wet, and terrified—clung to the rock.

In the morning, when the storm was over, a lifeboat came to the man's rescue. When he climbed into the boat, he collapsed, shivering from head to toe. One of his rescuers said, "Young man, you must have trembled all night long from cold and fear." Raising himself slightly, the rescued man replied, "Tremble? Yes, I did. But I knew that as long as I stayed put, I was safe. For the *rock* never trembled."

So it is with the Word of God. It is the sure rock on which we may take eternal refuge and safely build our lives. It never trembles in any circumstances—though, as we read it, *we* shall often tremble for the goodness of the Lord and the majesty of His might, revealed even in the most trying situations. Pure truth is infinitely attractive and endlessly serviceable.

Since the beginning of his rebellion, Satan has worked hard to misrepresent God through a crafty distortion of divine precepts. But in every generation the Lord has had faithful representatives to bear the banner of His eternal Word to the best of their knowledge and ability. Their cumulative witness has unfurled a progressive revelation of divine love even amid the raging storms of persecution and hatred of truth that mark the course of earth's history.

Moreover, the Spirit declared through the apostle Peter that Christ would return shortly after "the times of restoration of all things, which God has spoken by the mouth of all His holy prophets since the world began" (Acts 3:21, see context). More than a century and a half ago God raised up the Advent movement as His vehicle for this restoration of the gospel to its original purity, liberated from human theories that obscure the revelation of God's character and purposes. These restored truths, which have a vital bearing on the accurate presentation of the gospel, constitute pillars of our faith to bolster us for last-day trials and stabilize our standing in the ways of God.

Christ Himself, who is the way, the truth, and the life, tends the lamp of revelation to protect its integrity and foster its ever-increasing brightness for the benefit of all who wish to walk in its light. His special work on earth was to restore truth that had become dimmed, hidden behind the screen of human tradition. He testified, "To this end was I born, and for this cause came I into the world, that I should bear witness unto the truth. Every one that is of the truth heareth my voice" (John 18:37, KJV).

> Christ is the author of all truth. Every brilliant conception, every thought of wisdom, every capacity and talent of men, is the gift of Christ. He borrowed no new ideas from humanity, for He originated all. But when He came to earth He found the bright gems of truth which He had entrusted to man all buried up in superstition and tradition. Truths of most vital importance were placed in the framework of error, to serve the purpose of the arch deceiver. . . . But Christ swept away erroneous theories of every grade. No one save the

> world's Redeemer had power to present the truth in its primitive purity, divested of the error that Satan had accumulated to hide its heavenly beauty. . . . The work of Christ was to take the truth of which the people were in want, and separate it from error and present it free from the superstitions of the world, that the people might accept it on its own intrinsic and eternal merit. He dispersed the mists of doubt, that the truth might be revealed and shed distinct rays of light into the darkness of men's hearts.
>
> The truth came from His lips clothed in new and interesting representations that gave it the freshness of a new revelation. . . . His words came with an earnestness and assurance appropriate to their importance and the momentous consequences involved in their reception or rejection.[1]

Fresh insights for this generation

A book on doctrinal fundamentals risks being a droning exercise in self-affirmation or a bulkhead of sternly defended dogma reared on the coast of impervious tradition. Yet, it also carries the potential of insights that further illuminate long-cherished truths that have yielded rich benefit to God's people in former days. We should therefore reverently expect God to reveal more of His gracious and glorious purposes as we advance toward the day of His return. This does not call for efforts to conjure up some new thing, so that "each of you has a psalm, has a teaching, has a tongue, has a revelation" (1 Cor. 14:26). But it does mean realizing that Jesus wishes to shine forth with undimmed splendor into our hearts and guide us into practical, pertinent applications of unchanging truth that has hidden reserves of power to bless each generation according to their peculiar circumstances and fresh challenges.

It would be a great disservice to the Advent message, established in Scripture and confirmed by the Spirit of Prophecy, to suggest that any portion of it is declining in relevance. But it would be a nearly equal disservice to suppose that our vision has taken in the full glory and richest implications of the truth Christ commissions us to promulgate. Eternity itself will not suffice to exhaust the treasures of divine revelation, and we need not flatter ourselves that we have little more to learn (see Ps. 119:18, 96; Rom. 11:33-36; Col. 2:2, 3).[2] So, a study of fundamental doctrines holds the prospect of being far more than a refresher course or an academic drill. Rightly pursued, such study will enrich our walk with God. This is especially true when we include prophecy in our research. Why? Because prophecy illuminates the time-transcending will and character of God. It magnifies Christ as One whose infinitely loving purposes shall gloriously prevail and whose promises shall be bountifully fulfilled for all who believe and obey His Word. Such study cultivates intimacy with God and transformation into His likeness. To this end He gave us Scripture.

While few are called upon to be trailblazers to new truths, we are all bidden to let the truth blaze its way into our inmost being and make us burning and shining lights for the Lord. Commissioned to be repairers of the breach and restorers of paths to dwell in, God's final remnant must be prepared to bring forth from the treasury of His Word things new and old—materials that are of enduring power to rear a mansion of character that no forces of modernism, no assaults of adversity, and no arts of seduction can endanger.

It is the prayerful hope of this writer that all who read the following pages will not only have their faith affirmed but also expanded and invigorated. May the reader perceive new force and beauty in "the word of the Lord [which] endures forever" and makes us one with Him, according to the will of Christ (see 1 Pet. 1:25; John 17:17-26).

---

1. Ellen G. White, *That I May Know Him* (Hagerstown, Md.: Review and Herald, 1964), 207. This comment on the indispensability of doctrinal truth is corroborated in such passages as John 8:31-36; 2 John 9; 10; Rev. 19:13; 22:18, 19.

2. See also White, *Testimonies to Ministers and Gospel Workers* (Nampa, Idaho: Pacific Press, 1967), 111-119.

CHAPTER ONE

CHRIST IS ALL MY RIGHTEOUSNESS

Lonely, tired, and dusty, Dwain trudged along the road, rippling off pensive melodies on his bamboo flute. From time to time, he stooped over to pick up a can or other piece of roadside litter and toss it into a gunny sack roped to his waist. Dwain put food in his stomach by foraging for edible plants and by appearing at campsites that issued smoke carrying the savor of good cooking; his gaunt cheeks bespoke a need that kindhearted campers generally met. He supplemented his livelihood by sifting through the county dump for books, food, and clothes after emptying his sack into that putrid horn of plenty.

A drop-out in search of life's meaning, Dwain lived as a squatter in one of the most beautiful regions of the West Coast, among the giant redwoods. At night he could hear the mighty waves of the Pacific Ocean surging with steady rhythm along the shore. Often he would gaze with wonder upon the stars that shone through the swaying lacework of the evergreens beneath which he dwelt. But his heart knew no peace, no sense of connection to anything. He felt nothing but a gnawing sense of incompleteness—a desperate lack of righteousness.

It puzzled Dwain that so often he thought of this word, *righteousness*. After all, it hadn't been a central idea in his upbringing, which was totally secular. His moral foundation was tenuous and rife with inconsistencies. Bible teachings were for him a completely unexplored territory. Yet this idea of needing righteousness persisted. Dwain's collection of trash along the roadside was his attempt at making some modest contribution to society. Yet he sensed that all the broken beer bottles and crushed soda cans he picked up could not gain for him one jot of that poignantly elusive quality, that intangible jewel called righteousness. Somehow the thought of going through life without it seemed unacceptable to him. He saw righteousness as harmony with the cosmic mind, attunement to the fundamental laws of being. Why, he thought, live in discord with ultimate reality?

One day, while researching this subject in the philosophy section of a San Francisco library, he came across a translation of an ancient Egyptian poem. Though the poem was reputedly thirty-two hundred years old, Dwain felt it contemporary with his own experience. A section of the poem went something like this:

I sit by the fertile riverbed and weep
Because I am barren within.
My heart bears no sweet fruit,
Only thorns of bitterness and pain.
The birds sing happily
And gladden innocent ears,
But I groan because I can give no joy.
Oh, how can I know peace?
Will my heart ever be clean?
Who will stretch forth a healing rod
To take away my clinging evil?
I can find no joy if righteousness
Cannot dwell in my depths.
But, as a stranger to myself,
I know not how it may;

So I sit on the lush riverbanks and weep
For the dry reeds that rustle
In the parched gullies of my heart.

What is the origin of this mysterious craving for righteousness that Dwain and the unknown Egyptian poet experienced—indeed, that people in every nation and of every religion in all ages have known?

Jesus declared, " 'Blessed are those who hunger and thirst for righteousness, for they shall be filled' " (Matt. 5:6). Evidently, we're not born righteous. Even the desire for it is implanted by a source outside of ourselves.

The meaning of *righteousness*

What is righteousness? In the Old Testament, the Hebrew word is *tsedaka*, meaning rightness, justice, rectitude. It comes from the root word *tsadak*—to be right or be made right, to cleanse or to clear. The equivalent Greek word, used in the New Testament, is *dikaiosune*, which means equitable, innocent, holy, just.

Essentially, then, righteousness is right doing. And only those who are right with God can do right. It's indispensable to realize this. Paul affirms, " 'There is none righteous, no, not one' " (Rom. 3:10). Our best efforts to live a morally sound life fail dismally. With words that slice through our complacency like an Arctic blast, Isaiah wrote, "We are all like an unclean thing, and all our righteousnesses are like filthy rags; we all fade as a leaf, and our iniquities, like the wind, have taken us away" (Isa. 64:6).

Isaiah's words constitute a disturbingly factual diagnosis—and an absolutely necessary one. They force us to abandon all efforts to establish our own version of righteousness and direct our sight to its true source (see Rom. 9:30–10:4). When we know what absolutely won't work, then we are more open to trying what will.

Righteousness is not a quality that we can possess apart from a personal connection with God. It is not just an extracted dose of moral vigor that God gives us like an injection to ward off evil and infuse goodness. Jeremiah declared, " 'Behold the days are coming,' says the Lord, 'that I will raise to David a Branch of righteousness. . . . Now this is His name by which He will be called: THE LORD OUR RIGHTEOUSNESS.' " (Jer. 23:5, 6).

Christ is not just the source and supply of righteousness; *He is righteousness itself.* When we accept Him as our Savior, Christ credits all His righteousness to us as a gift (see Rom. 5:15-21). He gives Himself with this gift and becomes to us experientially "wisdom from God—and righteousness and sanctification, and redemption," that our glory should be in God and not in ourselves (see 1 Cor. 1:30, 31). "The righteousness of God is embodied in Christ. We receive righteousness by receiving Him."[1]

These straightforward texts make it as clear as can be: (1) Human beings cannot become righteous on their own. (2) Righteousness is an outcome of the new birth, resulting from acceptance of Christ as Savior. This revelation rules out the false concept of obtaining righteousness by works or as a reward for moral determination and fortitude on our part. Nothing less than harmony with the moral law of God constitutes righteousness, for, as David declared, "All Your commandments are righteousness" (Ps. 119:172; cp. Isa. 48:16-18).

> We have no righteousness of our own with which to meet the claims of the law of God. But Christ has made a way of escape for us. He lived on earth amid trials and temptation such as we have to meet. He lived a sinless life. He died for us, and now He offers to take our sins and give us His righteousness. If you give yourself to Him, and accept Him as your Saviour, then, sinful as your life may have been, for His sake you are accounted righteous. Christ's character stands in place of your character, and you are accepted before God just as if you had not sinned.
>
> More than this, Christ changes the heart. He abides in your heart by faith. You are to maintain this connection with Christ by faith and the continual surrender of your will to

Him; and so long as you do this, He will work in you to will and to do according to His good pleasure.[2]

Satan tries to confuse

With such full, all-sufficient blessings offered, it is easy to see why Satan has striven to confuse sincere minds about the nature, source, and effects of true righteousness. The greatest deception in the religious world is the notion that a general assent to the truth and partial conformity to it constitute righteousness. That is why this subject receives so much attention in Scripture, especially in the New Testament, and particularly in Paul's writings.

Under the Spirit's inspiration, Paul repeatedly emphasized that righteousness

- is a gift, and never a reward (Gal. 2:16-21; Eph. 2:8-12; Titus 3:5-7);
- does not come by the law, but by grace and grace alone (Gal. 2:21);
- comes to us solely through the atoning work of Christ (Rom. 5:17-21);
- is imputed and imparted to all who personally put faith in the saving merits of Christ's sacrifice (Rom. 3:21-26); and
- is the power of God that enables us to live in harmony with His law, by virtue of the new covenant (Rom. 8:1-4; 3:31).

Paul was not content with a veneer of righteousness, a delusive façade fabricated of the wood, hay, and stubble of self-merit. No, he wanted the righteousness that is of God by faith—the righteousness that is unto all and upon all who believe. And what clear-thinking person would want anything less, especially when it is freely available to all through the saving power of Calvary?

Righteousness is a gift of grace, and those who receive this gift will glow with love and gratitude to the divine Giver. Our appreciation of the gift will intensify as our fellowship with Him grows. Through Christ our righteousness, we will enjoy increasing intimacy with God and likeness to Him. This likeness is not an imitation but an assimilation and absorption of God into our own renewed hearts. The melding is complete through our steadfastly maintained choice to abide in Him. Thus God brings in His *everlasting righteousness* (Dan. 9:24)—everlasting by the mutual choice and desire of God and His redeemed. This is no shaky or variable condition. It is God-occupied, God-controlled, God-filled, and God-ordained.

In Ephesians 3:16-21, Paul describes the fullness of this experience as completely as human language can portray true spiritual life. Other master passages on righteousness by faith are Romans 3:21-26; Galatians 2:16-21; 3:1-29; 5:16-21; and Philippians 3:7-16. We should saturate our minds with these passages and meditate on them often. Our natural hearts do not readily receive these transcendent truths. We must pray that God will enlighten the eyes of our understanding to discern the glorious riches of righteousness by faith, which is "Christ in you, the hope of glory." This deeply internal blessing has its basis and perpetual support in the measureless kindness that God has extended to us. His goodness leads us to deepening repentance, faith in Christ, and submission of heart to Him. "When God pardons the sinner, remits the punishment he deserves, and treats him as though he had not sinned, He receives him into divine favor, and justifies him through the merits of Christ's righteousness."[3]

Those who are truly growing in grace and sanctification will have a constantly expanding appreciation of the justifying mercies of God in the work He wrought for us on Calvary. As our grasp of justification deepens, the fruit of this experience will be unto holiness. Therefore, justification by faith is the taproot of all spiritual development. Those who are growing in grace and in the knowledge of Christ do not have a diminishing sense of need for the justifying mercies of God. Rather, their sense of need and their desire for it progressively heightens. They place not a jot of confidence in their own spiritual development; instead, they rely solely on Christ's merits and keeping-power for their salvation.

True righteousness and self-righteousness are polar opposites. Self-righteousness is worse than a counterfeit; it is a counter *force* that wars against the righteousness of Christ—often while spuriously acting in His name. Self-righteousness flows from a fallen heart incapable of producing the genuine virtue. It is a self-deception. Until we are born again, righteousness is at best a grand abstraction, an unrealized ideal, "because the carnal mind is enmity against God; for it is not subject to the law of God, nor indeed can be" (Rom. 8:7).

But we must also face another common misconception about righteousness. It is the notion that Christ is our righteousness even if we ignore His will and ways, just so long as we profess faith in Him and have good feelings about the gospel.

> While God can be just, and yet justify the sinner through the merits of Christ, no man can cover his soul with the garments of Christ's righteousness, while practicing known sins, or neglecting known duties. God requires the entire surrender of the heart before justification can take place; and in order for man to retain justification, there must be continual obedience, through active, living faith that works by love and purifies the soul.[4]

In uniting our lives to Christ, we are imbued with His righteousness, which is a soul-force that enables us to walk as Christ walked, in joyful harmony with His will. When His grace reigns within, this is our happy, heaven-bound state. Overflowing with gladness because of God's plan and provision, the heavenly host proclaims, " 'Let us be glad and rejoice and give Him glory, for the marriage of the Lamb is come, and His wife has made herself ready.' And to her it was granted to be arrayed in fine linen, clean and bright, for the fine linen is the righteous acts of the saints" (Rev. 19:6-8). The righteous acts of the saints are simply the manifestation of God's indwelling presence, who declares, " 'Their righteousness is from Me' " (Isa. 54:17; cp. 61:10).

This righteousness emanates from the lives of those who possess it in a steady flow of godly attitudes, words, and deeds. Christ, the source of this supernatural blessing, is thereby glorified. "The work of righteousness shall be peace, and the effect of righteousness, quietness and assurance forever" (Isa. 32:17; cp. Phil. 1:10, 11; James 3:17, 18).

Look at righteousness in the abstract as an essentially legal condition of moral rectitude and it appears daunting and grim. Look at righteousness in the light of its exhibition on Calvary and it is attractive, compelling, and infinitely accessible. It is the joy of our hearts, for we have found Christ as our salvation and righteousness, which will never be removed so long as we abide in Him.

Christ "Himself bore our sins in His own body on the tree, that we, having died to sins, might live for righteousness—by whose stripes you were healed. For you were like sheep going astray, but have now returned to the Shepherd and Overseer of your souls" who leads you "in the paths of righteousness for His name's sake" (1 Pet. 2:24, 25; Ps. 23:3).

---

1. Ellen G. White, *Thoughts From the Mount of Blessing* (Nampa, Idaho: Pacific Press, 1956), 18.
2. White, *Steps to Christ* (Nampa, Idaho: Pacific Press, 1956), 62, 63.
3. White, *Selected Messages* (Hagerstown, Maryland: Review and Herald, 1958), 1:389.
4. Ibid., 366.

CHAPTER TWO

CREATION'S MEMORIAL DAY

I suppose everyone, including even the least religious person, has sometimes wondered, "Who am I? How did I get here? What are my roots and what is the purpose of my existence?" Noted American writer Alex Haley undertook the search for his ancestral origins and traced them back to about 1750, locating them in the Ivory Coast of Africa. He brilliantly narrated this historical adventure in his classic work *Roots*. But Haley could find only the outer branches of his ancestral tree. Who was his *primal* ancestor? Who was yours and mine?

Since the days of Charles Darwin, evolutionists have wanted us to believe that we are lucky descendants from an ape-like creature, which in turn evolved from more primitive forms of life that unexplainably modulated into complex symmetries over generations from the first mysteriously formed organic cell. However, science has never been able to defend this theory rationally. The "chain of evolution" consists of a series of missing links. The chain simply isn't there, and the mathematical probabilities lean staggeringly against the prospect of life and cosmic order emerging from unregulated chaos. Paleontological findings—ancient skeletal and leaf imprints in rocks—offer nothing to suggest a gradual transition from one species to another over the course of time. Instead, centuries of scientific observation demonstrate that each species and its generations of offspring remain true to the same type. Cats give birth to cats, dogs to dogs, and humans to humans.

From every scientific standpoint, the evidence of nature indicates creation by the direct, authoritative act of an infinite, supernatural intelligence. For example, the eye could not have developed by a gradual series of steps. Every part of the eye, including its connection to the visual cortex of the brain, is so delicately interrelated that it could not function correctly without all parts having come into place at the same time.

Darwin despaired when he thought about the eye, because evolution could never account for its existence. Its intricacy of design and function point overwhelmingly to the genius of a divine Creator. After his *Origin of Species* was published, Darwin wrote, "To suppose the eye, with all its inimitable contrivances for adjusting the focus to different distances, for admitting different amounts of light, and for the correction of spherical and chromatic aberration, could have been formed by natural selection, seems, I freely confess, absurd in the highest degree."

We can only agree with Darwin's statement and conclude that evolution is an unsubstantiated hypothesis, a myth espoused by scientists who cannot bring themselves to acknowledge the God who declares, " 'I have made the earth, and created man on it, I—My hands—stretched out the heavens, and all their host I have commanded' " (Isa. 45:12). We can rest assured that we are not outriders of some impersonal, unguided evolutionary process, but sons and daughters of God. Our roots are traceable not to mud or a monkey, but to the Maker of the universe.

Some eighty years ago, in the days of Model T Fords, a motorist's vehicle broke down on a country road. He glumly waited for someone to come along who could tow his car into town. But then another Model T came chugging up, a rare sight in that region. The driver and his party stepped out and asked the man if they could help. "You surely can," he said. "My car needs repair. Would you send help from the next town?" "Well, let's take a look," replied the other motorist. He took out a tool box, looked the disabled engine over, tinkered with it a while, gave the crank a few turns, and started the car. "How did you do it?" asked the astonished driver. The man answered, "Oh, I'm Henry Ford, I invented this thing."

If we want an explanation of life's origin, wouldn't it make sense to turn to the divine Inventor who made it all happen? Let's allow our minds to take a scriptural journey back to our origins.

The epic of Creation

According to Genesis chapters one and two, it took God only six literal days to create this solar system, including our world and the life it contains. Read the account slowly and carefully, starting with the words, "In the beginning God created the heavens and the earth" (Gen. 1:1). Allow yourself to visualize the beautiful epic of Creation that angels and other worlds witnessed (see Job 38:4-7). Consider the wonderfully logical sequence of unfolding events, and notice how each step prepared the way for the next.

Day 1: God forms the earth in empty space. It hangs steeped in darkness, a sphere of waters. Then the Spirit of God ruffles the quiet surface of the waters. A strong, musical voice rings out, " 'Let there be light!' " and light appears. Earth now stands like a giant embryo, full of mysterious promise and stark beauty.

Day 2: Once again God's voice rolls forth, now declaring, " 'Let there be a firmament [sky] in the midst of the waters, and let it divide the waters from the waters.' " In silent, steady procession great curtains of mist ascend to form a clear canopy of water covering earth's atmosphere. This prepares the way for the support of life.

Day 3: God now produces dramatic changes. He speaks the command, " 'Let the waters under the heavens be gathered together into one place, and let the dry land appear'; and it was so. And God called the dry land Earth, and the gathering together of waters He called Seas."

At first the land looks barren, but now the Master Artist speaks again, and every form of vegetation springs forth instantly. Grass, flowers, and majestic trees clothe the world in multicolored profusion, making it a richly variegated garden of delight. God surveys His handwork and sees that it is good.

Day 4: God chooses this day to create the sun and moon to provide the earth with light, warmth, and the regulation of tides. These heavenly bodies and the ones beyond stand as eternal markers of seasons, days, months, and years.

Day 5: Now the symphony of creation rises to new heights of intensity and richness. By His word God brings forth creatures that swim, splash, and play in seas lavishly decorated with coral, gems, and marine vegetation of every sort. Suddenly, the air comes alive with an enchanting variety of winged musicians—extravagantly colored, iridescent birds, gracefully chorusing their praise and joy as they dart about and perch in trees.

Day 6: God makes every land-dwelling creature, from the elephant to the ant, empowering each species to reproduce after its own kind. No laborious evolutionary process is involved. Each creature comes forth perfect, unique in appearance, mature in form and function. God creates all these wonders with delight and effortless ease.

But all that He has made thus far is a prelude to His crowning act of creation: humankind, whom He makes in His own image to share His own nature and characteristics: intelligence, love, benevolence, freedom of will, creative ability, moral perception, memory, expressive power—eternal, ever-expanding endowments. Because of the special relationship God intends to have with human beings, He follows a different course in creating Adam than He did for all the preceding creation. God *spoke* all the lower creatures into existence. But with His own hands God *sculpts* the first man from the elements of the earth and breathes the breath of His own life into him. Then He names him Adam. And not content to make a solitary human, God creates from Adam's side a suitable companion, Eve, Adam's equal in moral stature and intelligence.

God places these two children of His in the Garden of Eden, where they are to have the privilege of conversing daily with their Maker. From Him they are to learn about His character and laws, about the mysteries of the universe, and about the wonderful nature and potential of their own lives. They are to populate the earth with children who will share the delights of companionship with the Creator and His handiwork. And God appoints Adam and Eve the recreational work of tending their beautiful paradise garden.

Day 7: To enhance and guard the value of life for His new race of beings, God makes the Sabbath, thus providing them a weekly day of special intimacy with Him in whose presence they can find ever-increasing joy (see Pss. 16:11; 36:7-10).

At earth's creation God blessed and sanctified the seventh day as a divine appointment between Himself and His people forever. Established when the world was still perfect and unfallen, the Sabbath was not instituted as a response to sin or as a shadow of things to come but as a permanent memorial of God's creatorship and unchanging love for all. It testifies that rather than distancing Himself from His creation, God draws near it (see Rev. 4:11).

> The Sabbath and the family were alike instituted in Eden, and in God's purpose they are indissolubly linked together. On this day more than on any other, it is possible for us to live the life of Eden. It was God's plan for the members of the family to be associated in work and study, in worship and recreation, the father as priest of his household, and both father and mother as teachers and companions of their children. But the results of sin, having changed the conditions of life, to a great degree prevent this association. Often the father hardly sees the faces of his children throughout the week. He is almost wholly deprived of opportunity for companionship or instruction. But God's love has set a limit to the demands of toil. Over the Sabbath He places His merciful hand. In His own day He preserves for the family opportunity for communion with Him, with nature, and with one another.[1]

A haven in time

After Adam and Eve sinned, the Sabbath took on additional significance as an agency of God's re-creative power. It thus became a sign of His redeeming grace (Ezek. 20:12, 20). This experience is fully brought to life when we recognize that Christ, as the Lord of the Sabbath, is indeed Creator in partnership with His Father (Mark 2:27, 28; Col. 1:13-19). A haven in time from life's toil and care, the Sabbath beckons us to find refuge in Christ. For the believer, this experience permeates the entire week but finds special renewal on the Sabbath.

Sometimes one hears this rationalization: "I don't need to keep one particular day in seven for worship, my rest in Christ is perpetual. Consequently, I always have the Sabbath experience in my heart."

The fourth commandment answers this pious-sounding but flawed idea: " 'Remember the Sabbath day, to keep it holy. Six days you shall labor and do all your work, but the seventh day is the Sabbath of the Lord your God. In it you shall do no work.' " Right in the heart of the commandment that God spoke with His own lips and wrote with His own finger is a definite distinction between His Sabbath and the six working days of the week. God does not invite us to dissect or critique His law, but to believe and obey it. In so doing we experience the blessed fruits of harmonizing with His will, which aims at our happiness and sanctification. Sabbath observance does not confine our worship to one day. Rather, the true experience of Sabbath keeping imbues all our days with a heightened appreciation of God's constant companionship.

We experience renewal and re-creation when we come into worshipful, loving contact with God. On the Sabbath we lay aside our routine burdens and cares to take undistracted delight in His presence. For those who know the Lord, the Sabbath is no legalistic burden. Rather, they consider it as indispensable as dating is to a fervent courtship. You could never convince a lover that a date with his fiancée is legalism or a sign of excessive attachment. Nor could you persuade him that his love runs the risk of being limited to that one day, only to fade during the rest of the week. Rather, his appointed tryst will intensify the relationship for all future time. So it is with the

Sabbath. This special day perfumes the whole week with the aroma of God's presence. It vitalizes time with the kiss of eternity.

Isaiah promised that God's presence in the Sabbath will cause those who honor that day to ride upon the " 'heights of the earth' " and to be fed " 'with the heritage of Jacob your father' " (Isa. 58:14, RSV). That heritage is the bestowal of all God's promised blessings to His covenant-keeping people.

Anticipating the effects of the theory of evolution, the widespread contempt for divine law, and the general abandonment of simple faith in the Scriptures that would prevail in the last days, the Lord has sent a message specially formulated for earth's final days. This threefold message, recorded in Revelation 14:6-12, calls humanity back to the "faith which was once delivered unto the saints" (Jude 3, KJV). It is an imperative call to worship the Creator on His own terms and to break free from the tyranny of self-worship and subjection to unsanctified authorities in matter of conscience. God's admonition in this passage contains the very wording of the Sabbath commandment (cp. Rev. 14:7; Exod. 20:11).

Satan induces people to dismiss the Sabbath as antiquated ceremonialism or cramped legalism. Instead of honoring God's Sabbath, many, under the power of Satan's sophistries or the hallowed umbra of tradition, embrace Sunday, his counterfeit sabbath, for their day of rest. This error, when crystallized into a law directly countermanding the true Sabbath, will bring humanity to the ultimate test of their mettle. But more on this in coming chapters.

In the meanwhile, let us remember that one sentence of Scripture is worth infinitely more than ten thousand volumes of the most glittering fallacies. May we sincerely declare with David, "I love Thy commandments above gold; yea, above fine gold. Therefore I esteem all Thy precepts concerning all things to be right; and I hate every false way" (Ps. 119:127, 128, KJV).

Pauliasi's Sabbath

The life of Pauliasi Bunoa, a Fijian minister who earned the reputation for great scholarship and deep spirituality, beautifully illustrates this resolve. When shown the truth about the perpetuity of God's Ten Commandments, including the seventh-day Sabbath, Pauliasi became deeply distressed. But because he was an honest man, he prayerfully studied the issue through, accepted the Sabbath, and became a Seventh-day Adventist minister.

Pauliasi's former colleagues in the very conservative denomination in which he had previously ministered were incensed with him. Determined to alienate him from his new-found faith, they invited him to hear a prominent minister preach. Pauliasi went and listened carefully to the minister exalt Sunday and denounce the Sabbath.

When he had finished his sermon, the preacher came down the aisle to where Pauliasi was sitting. He said, "I am very sorry, Pauliasi, that you have turned away from the church that you have so long upheld and served as a preacher."

"I am sorry too," Pauliasi replied. "But the Bible has driven me to this decision."

"Didn't you understand my sermon this morning?" asked the missionary.

"Oh, yes, I understood," Pauliasi said. "But you gave only the words of human beings to support your arguments. You gave no texts from the Bible. Brother missionary, if you could give me just one 'Thus saith the Lord' commanding us to keep Sunday, I would come back to my old church at once."

The European missionary stood in silence. Then, under the inspiration of the Holy Spirit, Pauliasi said very humbly, "Brother missionary, you are not the judge over this Sabbath law, and neither am I. But if in the great day of judgment I am found to be wrong, I am going to appeal to Jehovah because He wrote with His own finger the Ten Commandments, the fourth of which says that the seventh day is the Sabbath, and we are commanded to keep it. And if found to be wrong, I will plead that the patriarchs and prophets of Old Testament times all taught the seventh-day Sabbath and kept it. And I will also appeal to the teachings of the Lord Jesus Christ, who on the mount said, 'Think not that I am come to destroy the law. . . . I am not come to destroy, but to fulfill.' And Jesus kept His Father's commandments, and rested on the holy Sabbath, and preached in the synagogues. And if I am found to be wrong, I will refer to the scriptural authority of the apostle Paul, who said of the law that it was holy, just, and good and who honored the Sabbath day by preaching in the synagogue, by the riverside, and to the Gentiles on that day.

"In short, if I am wrong, I will plead my case on the strength of the teachings of God, the patriarchs and prophets of Old Testament times, and Jesus, Paul, and the other apostles in New Testament times. But, brother missionary, if *you* are found to be wrong over this Sunday question, to what word and example of Bible characters or of God and His Son will *you* be able to appeal?"

The missionary had no answer. But those who listened to this exchange searched their hearts and the Bible, and many became Sabbath keepers.[2]

---

1. Ellen G. White, *Education* (Nampa, Idaho: Pacific Press, 1903), 250.

2. Eric B. Hare, *Fulton's Footprints in Fiji* (Nampa, Idaho: Pacific Press, 1985), 113, 114 (adapted).

CHAPTER THREE

I AM HIS AND HE IS MINE

Charlotte looked at the watercolor on her lap. It drew her into a beautiful sunlit glade carpeted with bluebells and ringed by a cypress forest whose luxuriant depths were a green palace to woodland fauna. The glade sloped toward a still pond at which a doe was raising her head as a gallant buck emerged from the woods, raptly fixing his eyes on her.

A flood of memories washed over Charlotte. Six years earlier Bryce had given her that enchanting picture with the following inscription on its back: "To my dearly beloved Charlotte, this drawing expresses something of the mystic wonder and radiant joy you bring into my life. May it set a seal forever to our mutual love. Your devoted Bryce."

They had always said this watercolor was their pictorial marriage license. But now Charlotte's tears splashed on the surface of the idyllic scene, first blurring and then washing its features away. The once-vivid buck became an indistinguishable blotch toward which the doe stared with pathetically pointless wonder—for nothing remained there to invite her attention but sullen mist.

And so had ended Charlotte and Bryce's life together. For Bryce had drifted into a private world of marijuana-smoking and endless production of watercolors depicting misty mountain scenes and remote horizons. He had less and less time for Charlotte. He had washed her out of his life, and now her tears unwillingly yet ineluctably dissolved his image, leaving only a residue of grief and sad memories. The painting, once offered as a pledge of perennial love, was now a smudged symbol of love abandoned, love displaced through absorption in a world of art that had become soulless and aloof.

Symbols can wear thin. Their meaning can become mired in forgetfulness and neglect. They can also become a cloak to conceal estrangement, apathy, or treason. A couple may have their marriage license framed and displayed proudly, while the marriage relation itself has no more spark than wet ashes. People may wear gold wedding rings and yet be adulterous in heart and practice. Some who salute a flag, sing a national anthem, and engage in other patriotic exercises betray the land to which they pay apparent homage. So, the exaltation of symbols often substitutes for true commitment and heartfelt allegiance.

In the Sabbath, God has given us more than a symbol—something far greater than a ceremonial observance. His weekly Sabbath is a memorial of His creatorship, a changeless testimony of the love that moves Him to seek fellowship with His creation. The Sabbath is like a fountain of eternity bursting forth at appointed intervals across the rough wilderness of time. It is a golden clasp that binds God's people to Himself. Therefore, if for us this sacred day is not imbued with a distinct sense of His eternal presence, its meaning dies. If we treat it with a casualness that lets outside influences distract us from fellowship with God, it becomes a sham. This day, then, becomes to us a bland custom—or even a yoke of bondage.

God didn't create the Sabbath to form a barrier. He meant it to foster intimacy between the intelligent beings He created and Himself. It is a gift of love, of covenantal union between God and His people. " ' "Hallow My Sabbaths, and they will be a sign between Me and you, that you may know that I am the Lord your God" ' "

(Ezek. 20:20). This sign is not a static image or a fleeting gesture; it is a weekly endowment of substantial time. Those who purposely and repeatedly spend time with someone provide persuasive evidence of loving regard for that chosen companion and a means of enriching the relationship.

Sealed in love

It was the amount of time King Solomon spent by choice with the Shulamite[1] woman that convinced her of his sincere attachment to her. Three times in the Song of Solomon, she affectionately declares, " 'My beloved is mine, and I am His' " (Song of Sol. 2:16; 6:3; 7:10). She also says, " 'He feeds his flock among the lilies.' " Lilies signify purity, beauty, delicacy, exalted life sustained in earthly settings. In form, lilies resemble cherishing hands shaped like an open chalice to lovingly contain and dispense blessings (see 1 Kings 7:26). This imagery points to seeking that which is pleasant, pure, and uplifting. It betokens the privileges of being heirs together of the grace of life with Christ. In a tide of inspiration that captures the essence of the nuptial union Christ establishes with His people, Solomon's betrothed declares, " 'Set me as a seal upon your heart, as a seal upon your arm' " (Song of Sol. 8:6).

Sealing, as presented in Scripture, is a profoundly life-transforming process. Applied physically, a seal stamps the surface of an object with the impression of its own image. A seal can mark an object without altering the essential character of that object. In its spiritual application, however, sealing involves a relational pact of mutual belonging, an internalizing of the properties of the sealing agent. Scripture makes this clear: "He who establishes us with you in Christ and has anointed us is God, who also has sealed us and given us the Spirit in our hearts as a guarantee" (2 Cor. 1:22). This sealing unites us to Christ in preparation for His coming and enables us to represent and serve Him faithfully while we wait (Eph. 4:30-32).

In addition to sealing us, the Holy Spirit also inscribes the law upon our hearts. Only God can accomplish this change. He does it by first giving us a new heart that delights to obey Him (see Ezek. 36:26-29). David's petitionary vow reflects the attitude of God's people toward His law: "Give me understanding and I shall keep thy law; yea, I shall observe it with my whole heart. Make me to go in the path of thy commandments, for therein do I delight" (Ps. 119:33, 34, KJV). The law doesn't detract from the peace of those who serve God; rather, it illuminates the way of peace, for it reveals the inner workings of harmony with God.

Those who love God's law on these terms need offer no apology to the world for their commitment. They recognize that a love for God's law is a perpetual fruit of true conversion. Christ, their Redeemer and Lawgiver, has imparted to them the new-covenant experience of the inscribing of His law in their hearts, which have been renewed through the power of the gospel (Ezek. 36:26; Heb. 8:10-12).

Recognizing that the world is always at variance with divine law, the converted do not seek theological endorsement from the world's great teachers of religion. However, neither does their liberty in Christ lead them to make boastful claims about being patterns of perfection or embodiments of holiness (see Ps. 119:73, 77, 80). Those who are most truly obedient to God have a very humble and contrite attitude set in an atmosphere of hope and devotion to God. Their constant petition is "Open my eyes that I might behold wondrous things in Your law." They pray that the eyes of their understanding be enlightened to discern more fully the wonders of God's everlasting gospel (see Ps. 119:18; Eph. 1:18).

In their ignorance, many scorn God's moral law as a yoke of bondage. But those who love the Lord keep His commandments (see John 14:15; 15:10; 1 John 2:3-5; 5:2, 3), recognizing that they are an expression of His character, a beautifully codified statement of how divine love implanted in human hearts reveals itself in our relations with God and humankind. Thus the voice of God decrees: " 'Bind up the testimony, seal the law among my disciples' " (Isa. 8:16). This text plainly shows that the law *in its totality* is a seal that God places upon His people.

God's Sabbath, His seal

Extending from this function of the law in the heart as a divine seal, the Sabbath takes on special significance. "The fourth commandment is the only one of the ten in which are found the name and the title of the Lawgiver. It is the only one that shows by whose authority the law is given. Thus it contains the seal of God, affixed to His law as evidence of its authenticity and binding force."[2]

"Pointing to God as the Maker of the heavens and the earth, [the Sabbath] distinguishes the true God from all false gods. All who keep the seventh day signify by this act that they are worshipers of Jehovah. Thus the Sabbath is the sign of man's allegiance to God as long as there are any upon the earth to serve Him"[3]

God denotes the Sabbath as a sign between Himself and His people (Exod. 31:13, 17; Ezek. 20:12, 20). It is revealing that the word for *sign* as used in these passages is embedded in the very word *Sabbath*. The Hebrew word *oth* means "seal," "mark," "insignia of ownership." Some scholars have suggested that in composite etymology, the word *Sabbath* means "sign of the bountiful Father." Fatherhood implies creatorship; therefore the word *Sabbath* inherently suggests that it is the sign of the Creator who generously brings forth beauty and perfection in all His works.

Moreover, *oth* especially signifies "that which is given by one who speaks in the name of God, in witness of some disputed truth, or as a token of some future event."[4] This observation is significant considering that

- God appointed the Sabbath as a witness of His creatorship. We are to take what He reveals in His Word about having created the world in six literal days and having rested the seventh in faith and reverent acceptance of His authority and veracity.
- The Sabbath is vigorously opposed by many who reject the Creation account and others who want to relegate this day to the status of a Jewish ceremonial law despite its being placed at the heart of the Decalogue and having been established before the nations were formed.

• Prophecy also features the Sabbath as an issue over which Satan will arouse massive intolerance and persecution through forcing the observance of an apostate day of worship in place of God's memorial day. So, in a prophetic sense, the Sabbath constitutes God's end-time seal to distinguish His commandment-keeping people from those who accept the authority of tradition and human edicts above divine law. Because the Sabbath is scorned and rationalized away by the worldly-wise, it operates in a special sense as a sign of loyalty to God to distinguish His people from the idolatrous and unbelieving. (We will see more about this in the next chapter.)

If people had kept the Sabbath from the creation of our world as God intended, it would have been impossible for anyone to drift into idolatry, atheism, or irreverence. The Sabbath stands not only as a memorial of God's perfect work, but as a day of delight and intimate fellowship with our Lifegiver and Sustainer.

Why does a day matter?

Some ask what difference a day makes—as though this question were a very perceptive challenge. The answer takes us back to the specifics of God's Word. He declares that the seventh day is the Sabbath of the Lord because it memorializes His creation of our world in six days. By beginning His fourth commandment with the word *remember*, God signified that He instituted the Sabbath *before* He enunciated the Ten Commandments on Sinai. He gave the Sabbath to Adam and Eve in the Garden of Eden prior to their sin. In the wilderness, even before proclaiming the Ten Commandments, the Lord fed His people manna, which He gave in double measure on the sixth day to spare them the labor of gathering food on the Sabbath. By this miraculous provision He accentuated the sanctity of the seventh day above all the other days of the week.

Specifically then, God gave us the Sabbath to keep us mindful of His creatorship and His loving interest in having enhanced, undivided communion with us whom He created in His own image on the sixth day of Creation week. His explanation for giving us the Sabbath is simple, clear, and reasonable.

Who, then, are we to critique God's ways? Why scorn or depreciate His periodic gift of time that keeps us freshly and forever linked with Him? No one has ever benefited from reasoning away God's commands, negating His promises, or denying His prophecies. In light of God's specifying the Sabbath as a sign between Him and His people, those who observe it with their whole hearts thereby plainly show their allegiance to Him. For all who keep the Sabbath as God intended, it is a day of delight—for they find the Lord's promised presence in those sacred hours. On this day God draws near to His people and lifts them to heights of advanced spiritual refreshment known only to those who embrace His stated will (see Isa. 58:12-14). They enjoy contemplating His marvelous works in connection with the wonders of His redeeming love (see Pss. 19; 111).

What a mistake it would be to reason away the blessing that God holds forth to us with loving entreaty. The courtesy of His appeal, the cordiality of His invitation, in no way lessens its authority or excuses our unresponsiveness. For sensitive, worshipful believers, Christ's invitation is equivalent to a command—which they promptly obey with delight. For His commands are a loving call to follow Him into realms of grace and glory.

Ever mindful that Christ is the Lord of the Sabbath day, the redeemed hold appreciatively in view that their Creator is also their Redeemer and Sanctifier. They know from Scripture and the revelation of God's Spirit that redemption is a divinely initiated and consummated work of recreating fallen humans into the image of God (see Ps. 51:6-10; Eph. 4:22-24). They appreciate the Sabbath as a special weekly refuge from temporality—particularly in light of God's calling the Sabbath a sign of His power to sanctify all who worship Him in spirit and in truth.

These believers do not worship the *Sabbath* but the *Lord* of the Sabbath. In that process they come to bear a likeness to Christ in character, and thus, fully settled into the truth intellectually and spiritually, they receive His seal. They have entered into His rest and are not ashamed to worship Him in harmony with His law and testimony. For them the Sabbath is an active pledge of allegiance to their Life-giver and Sustainer, to whose workmanship they joyfully yield their lives. And He is not ashamed to confess them as His own before His Father and the angels. For He has not only sealed them with His own law and love, but has also set them as a seal and signet upon His own heart, crowning them with royal favor as His diadems of delight and vessels of honor.

Neither time nor trials shall ever break that precious bond of union. "For thus says the Lord: 'To [those] who keep My Sabbaths, and choose what pleases Me, and hold fast My covenant, even to them I will give in My house and within My walls a place and a name better than that of sons and daughters; I will give them an everlasting name that shall not be cut off. Also the sons of the foreigner who join themselves to the Lord, to serve Him, and to love the name of the Lord, to be His servants—everyone who keeps from defiling the Sabbath, and holds fast My covenant—even them I will bring to My holy mountain, and make them joyful in My house of prayer' " (Isa. 56:4-7).

He shall make His faithful children all glorious within and bring them to His palace—not as tourists herded through its halls for a brief glimpse of His glory, but as royal residents, sealed for time and eternity to their Creator, Redeemer, and King. No tears of abandonment or betrayal will ever dim their future. It will always be luminous with the smiles of well-remembered, never-fading love.

---

1. The words *Solomon* and *Shulamite* both derive from the same root word (*shalom*), which means "peace," "reciprocal attachment," "fellowship," "responsiveness," and the like. Typologically, Solomon's betrothal to the Shulamite points to the perfect peace that we have with God through our Lord Jesus Christ (see Rom. 5:1; Luke 2:14). This peace signifies not only the end of all strife, but also the forming of happy, prosperous, and secure relations, the satisfactions of which never end.

2. Ellen G. White, *Patriarchs and Prophets* (Nampa, Idaho: Pacific Press, 1958), 307.

3. *Ibid.*

4. William Wilson, *Old Testament Word Studies* (Peabody, Mass.: Hendrickson Publishers, nd.), 394.

CHAPTER FOUR

A TIME FOR JOY

One of the ironies of our modern world is that no previous generation has had so many inventions that enable people to accomplish in minutes or hours tasks that once would have taken them several days or months to perform. Sociologists estimate that workers in the high-tech/industrialized world now have 40 leisure hours a week. As never before, people are free to pursue their favorite pastimes. Yet, they seem to find less and less time for God. Few, even among religious persons, have embraced the blessing of keeping a whole 24-hour weekly Sabbath with full commitment to its purpose.

Foreseeing this trend toward worldliness, Paul spoke of people in the last days as being "lovers of pleasure rather than lovers of God," "having the form of godliness, but denying its power" (2 Tim. 3:4, 5). As a result of all this indulgence, society has grown weary, jaded, dissatisfied. Depression has been on the rise since 1915. It is the most common mood disorder in the modern world. Many suffer from a profound sense of estrangement from themselves, from one another, and from the very Source of their being. They are alienated from God (see Eph. 4:17, 18).

All this stems from humanity's pandemic ignorance of its origin. Few fully believe that God created our first ancestors expressly in His own image. Universities teach that this fundamental revelation is a myth. Many theologians and pastors in Christendom treat the Genesis account of human origins as little more than an allegory, a kindergarten version of stupendous cosmological facts that civilization in its infancy was too primitive to understand.

Having discarded belief in the literalness of the accounts of Creation and humanity's Fall as recorded in the early chapters of Genesis, people are now free to devise endless hypotheses about their origin and destiny. This wide-open speculation has left the modern world without spiritual bearings. It's no wonder, then, that so many people feel spiritual nausea and malaise. To them, life resembles a restless sea, perpetually casting up mire and dirt. No haven of rest is in sight, no harbor of gracious experience. So, whether on water skis or in a line of starving refugees; whether sipping daiquiris or scrambling for ditch-water to slake blistering thirst, bewildered and deceived humanity moves toward the abysmal unknown.

How different it is for those who know and love their Creator and Redeemer! For them, instead of being dreary vagabondage, life is a purposeful pilgrimage, a heavenward odyssey that puts a spring in their step and a song in their heart. Though oft sorely beset with trials, such pilgrims find daily refreshment in communion with their Lord through prayer and the study of Scripture. Nourished within, they rest in the promises of His Word and rejoice in His precepts. Vitalized by ever-strengthening bonds of union with Christ, they are filled with peace beyond understanding. In His presence they find fullness of joy, and at His right hand pleasures forevermore. This is not high-flown rhetoric or pious fantasy, but the joyful reality of their lives.

A weekly haven

To enrich their daily rest in Christ, God's commandment-keeping people also enjoy a weekly haven of rest, a sanctuary in time for a divinely-appointed tryst with their Lord. It is the seventh-day Sabbath. Keeping the Sabbath is no more of a burden for those who love their Redeemer-King—it is no more tainted with legalism or pigeonholed devotion—than is a weekly date between busy lovers. When two people who love each other spend choice time together, the rest of the week bears a special glow of treasured memories and a heightened sense of connection and accord.

Viewed in this light, the Sabbath becomes an extension and enrichment of our daily walk with the Lord. It is not catch-up time that attempts to compensate for our neglect of Him during the week, but a fragrant heavenly bloom that crowns with special delight the week's unfolding intimacies. It is no more a yoke of bondage than is a honeymoon for two people euphorically in love. So, the Sabbath not only marks the origin and end of time, it also braids eternity into our all-too-earth-bound calendars. It helps us transcend our ephemeral routines and rise above our self-serving agendas.

Though written in honor of Sunday rather than of the true, seventh-day Sabbath, the following lines by the poet George Herbert express a vivid appreciation for God's weekly day of rest:

O day most calm, most bright,
The fruit of this, the next world's bud,
Th' endorsement of supreme delight,
Writ by a friend, and with His blood;
The couch of time; care's balm and bay:
The week were dark, but for thy light:
Thy torch doth show the way.
Thou are a day of mirth:
And where the weekly days trail on ground,
Thy flight is higher, as thy birth.
O let me take thee at a bound,
Leaping with thee from seven to seven,
Till that we both, being tossed from earth,
Fly hand in hand to heaven![1]

(In George Herbert's day, "mirth" signified innocent delight rather than giddy merriment.)

A growing experience

Sabbath observance is an experience we grow into. Guided by Scripture, any interested person can make a healthy start as a Sabbath keeper. But, like a godly marriage, Sabbath keeping grows richer as our relationship with Christ, Lord of Creation, develops.

In almost rhapsodic imagery, Isaiah speaks of the manifold blessings the Sabbath brings those who observe it in harmony with God's purpose:

> "If you turn away your foot from the Sabbath, from doing your pleasure on My holy day, and call the Sabbath a delight, the holy day of the Lord honorable, and shall honor Him, not doing your own ways, nor finding your own pleasure, nor speaking your own words, then you shall delight yourself in the Lord; and I will cause you to ride upon the high hills of the earth, and feed you with the heritage of Jacob your father. The mouth of the Lord has spoken" (Isa. 58:13, 14).

These two verses are spiritual keys to unlock the treasure house of true Sabbath observance. First, they point to the depth of the new-covenant experience. Humans can turn their feet away from the Sabbath (cease trampling it underfoot as common time) only if they value personal fellowship with God such as Enoch had. Plainly, God differentiates between the Sabbath and the other days of the week. He intended the day of rest to provide His people with an opportunity at each week's close to renew and extend their fellowship with Him. This is why He instructs us to desist from secular conversation and activities for the entire seventh day. He wants to clear the way for us to have undivided joy in Him. Consequently, it is apparent that in God's mind the Sabbath is not a ceremonial observance but a relational link between Himself and His people.

Moreover, this passage emphasizes our experiencing on the Sabbath elevated personal pleasure in the *Lord* rather than in *rituals.* When we keep the Sabbath as God intends, He prepares a weekly banquet for the soul and lifts us far beyond earth's dim atmosphere to the heights of heavenly bliss. Once we enter this experience, we can readily discern what factors are conducive to true Sabbath observance. This is not a matter of ecclesiastical rules and regulations, but of divine guidance through the Word. Christ offers us the anointing of His Spirit to teach us how to apply the general principles of truth to the particular circumstances of life (see 1 John 2:27).

Sometimes people ask, "Has the church drawn up a list of do's and don'ts for Sabbath keeping so that we can avoid making mistakes?" We can certainly respect the desire of such persons to please God. However, the Lord has not given the church the onerous task of being conscience and lifestyle monitor for anyone. It is the personal responsibility of all believers to grow up "to the measure of the stature of the fullness of Christ" without shifting the burden on others to tell them what they may or may not do on the Sabbath. In this matter, as in all others revealed in Scripture, Jesus' counsel is, " 'What saith the law? How readest thou?' "

Scripture identifies certain activities that constitute a clear violation of the Sabbath because they trample underfoot the sacred purpose of the time and depreciate its value. Examples include engaging in commerce, dreaming about one's own plans, taking part in secular conversation and pastimes, and working at mundane tasks whether for a livelihood or one's personal convenience (see Neh. 13:15-22; Jer. 17:19-22). Such activities obstruct the full, unfettered enjoyment of God's holy day. We must remember that the Lord draws near to His people on the Sabbath. He intends this day to provide time for intimacy and communion with Him. If we really believe that God is seeking a closer fellowship with us during the Sabbath hours, then how thoughtless we would be to squander its hours on secular business.

Apprehensive of fellowship

When Sabbath keeping was new to me as a young Christian, I soon became a little apprehensive of having extensive fellowship with other Sabbath keepers after church. It wasn't because they were disagreeable or I was antisocial. Rather, I discovered that for all too many, the Sabbath quickly became Saturday once church was over. Every topic of the world was open for discussion, with the possible exception of the lottery and the latest political scandal.

Ellen White, whose walk with the Lord was constantly maturing, wrote: "I was shown that there has been too much slackness with regard to the Sabbath."[2] Carelessness in Sabbath keeping is a sign of spiritual insensitivity.

> Great blessings are enfolded in the observance of the Sabbath, and God desires that the Sabbath day shall be to us a day of joy . . . [to] direct our minds to Him as the true and living God, and that through knowing Him we may have life and peace. . . . The Sabbath is a golden clasp that unites God and His people.[3]

Devout believers take Christ as their example in everything. Let's consider, then, how Christ, the Lord of the Sabbath, modeled the keeping of His own day. He performed acts that ended suffering and restored health. These were not routine services like weeding a neighbor's garden or painting a shut-in's fence. Such thoughtful deeds can be performed on other days. Christ devoted the Sabbath to actions that directly linked people with God and banished affliction. For Him it was not a day of idleness or of casual good-will. It had a well-directed purpose at all times: the glory of God and the restoration of humanity.

Jesus' guide to Sabbath keeping was Scripture, not artificial rabbinic codes. Modern preachers often echo the old Pharisaic allegation that Christ broke the Sabbath (see John 5:18). In reality, however, Jesus never did. He chose to heal the afflicted on the Sabbath not only to address their immediate need, but also to set people free from the false views of God and His law that clustered like barnacles around the Sabbath. It was Satan's strategy to turn God's day of delight into a day of dread. Not only did the religious leaders of Christ's time encrust the Sabbath with cumbersome requirements, they also disallowed the very works that are appropriate on that day (see Matt. 12:1-14; John 5:1-20).

When facing His accusers, Jesus asked, " 'Which of you convicts me of sin?' " (John 8:46). He could factually declare, " 'I have kept My Father's commandments, and abide in His love' " (John 15:10). So, rather than desecrating the Sabbath, Jesus, the Lord of the Sabbath because He is the Lord of Creation, restored and exemplified the true meaning of His holy day. He put the whole matter into perspective by reminding His accusers that " 'the Sabbath was made for man, and not man for the Sabbath' " (Mark 2:27). He showed that Sabbath observance was not an obstacle course intended to weed out religious weaklings or a medium for the exhibition of superior piety. Rather, He demonstrated that the Sabbath is paved with love, pavilioned with grace, and garnished with accents of beauty. Christ's manner of keeping this day was a richly textured re-echo of His invitation to " 'come to Me, all you who labor and are heavy laden, and I will give you rest' " (Matt. 11:28).

Preparation for the Sabbath

To obtain the full benefit of the Sabbath, we need to prepare for it throughout the week. Foremost in our preparation must be the daily practice of the laws of Christ's kingdom—the royal law of liberty, love, and uncompromising honesty. Every day we should let God's light shine through us in good works, that others may glorify Him. We should practice kindness in our homes. Then, when the Sabbath comes, we will not have to don a mask of pretended spirituality. Joined in the bonds of mutual love and respect, the whole family can joyfully welcome the Sabbath together.

With the help of such texts as Exodus 16; 34:21; Nehemiah 13:15-22; Amos 8:5; and Luke 23:52-56 and the valuable guidelines given in the Spirit of Prophecy chapter "The Observance of the Sabbath,"[4] we discover the following directions for making the most effective preparation for the Sabbath:

• Pray during the week that the sanctification of the Sabbath may rest upon you.
• Immerse yourself daily in God's Word.
• Avoid overworking during the week so that the Sabbath doesn't become a day of exhaustion and sleep.
• Let mind and body be withdrawn from worldly business before the Sabbath begins.
• Have special Sabbath clothing (tasteful but not opulent) that you wear only on the Lord's day.
• Complete cooking, cleaning, and shopping well before sunset on Friday.
• Make amends with one another for any conflicts or misunderstandings that have arisen during the week.
• Put secular papers and journals out of sight and turn off the radio and TV. In short, clear the way for God and angels to come to your home.

To get the full benefit of the Sabbath, begin and end the sacred hours with prayer, praise, singing, and Scripture reading. Get to bed early so that you can be well rested for church service. And attend Sabbath School and church. Remember, God gave the Sabbath as a day of *holy convocation*, and Jesus customarily went to God's house on the Sabbath (see Lev. 23:3; Luke 4:16).

After the church service, you might have additional fellowship with like-minded believers for spiritual edification, study the Scripture with interested persons, visit the sick, join a sunshine band and sing to shut-ins, spend time in nature with your family to contemplate God's creative power and love, or spend personal time alone with God. Remember also that the Sabbath provides opportunity for acts of mercy and benevolence toward lonely, afflicted, and destitute people. Consider both Christ's example of Sabbath keeping and Isaiah 58:6-14, the charter for God's remnant church in all ages but especially at the end of time, when human need for love and compassion is at its most critical point.

For those who love the Lord, such activities will be richly fulfilling. But for those who do not truly know God, the Sabbath hours will hang heavy and their termination will be a tremendous relief. This is a sad loss and a sign of spiritual bankruptcy. The way we spend the Sabbath is an index to our spiritual development.

Getting the most from the church service

Many believers are quite ambivalent about regular attendance at church services on the Sabbath. But consider how enthusiastic the early church was about coming together in corporate worship (see Acts 2–5). They didn't regard church attendance as a task but as a festival for the soul, a time of glowing communion with God and edifying fellowship with each other. They were vividly mindful of God's presence in all their assemblies. If we cherished that same awareness today, how much more gratifying church fellowship would be—especially if we excluded all worldly elements from our worship!

> The church of God below is one with the church of God above. Believers on the earth and the beings in heaven who have never fallen constitute one church. Every heavenly intelligence is interested in the assemblies of the saints who on earth meet to worship God. . . .
>
> Let us remember that our praises are supplemented by the choirs of the angelic host above.
>
> The temple of God is opened in heaven, and the threshold is flushed with the glory which is for every church that will love God and keep His commandments. We need to study, to meditate, and to pray. Then we shall have spiritual eyesight to discern the inner courts of the celestial temple. We shall catch the themes of song and thanksgiving of the heavenly choir round about the throne. When Zion shall arise and shine, her light will be most penetrating, and precious songs of praise and thanksgiving will be heard in the assemblies of the saints. Murmuring and complaining over little disappointments and difficulties will cease. As we apply the golden eyesalve we

shall see the glories beyond. Faith will cut through the heavy shadow of Satan, and we shall see our Advocate offering up the incense of His own merits in our behalf. When we see this as it is, as the Lord desires us to see it, we shall be filled with a sense of the immensity and diversity of the love of God.

God teaches that we should assemble in His house to cultivate the attributes of perfect love. This will fit the dwellers of earth for the mansions that Christ has gone to prepare for all who love Him. There they will assemble in the sanctuary from Sabbath to Sabbath, from one new moon to another, to unite in loftiest strains of song, in praise and thanksgiving to Him who sits upon the throne, and to the Lamb for ever and ever.[5]

---

1. George Herbert, *The Temple and a Priest to the Temple* (London: E. P. Dutton, 1908), 72, 74.

2. Ellen G. White, *Testimonies for the Church* (Nampa, Idaho: Pacific Press, 1948), 1:531.

3. Ibid., 6:349, 351.

4. Ibid., 6:349-368.

5. Ibid., 6:366, 367, 368.

CHAPTER FIVE

UNALLOYED GOOD NEWS

"I saw another angel flying in the midst of heaven, having the everlasting gospel to preach to those who dwell on the earth—to every nation, tribe, tongue, and people—saying with a loud voice, 'Fear God and give glory to Him, for the hour of His judgment has come; and worship Him who made the heaven and earth, the sea and springs of water.' " —Rev. 14:6, 7

God has not committed the work of preaching the gospel primarily to angels. He has entrusted this task to human beings. Without doubt, holy angels are vitally involved in directing this work and guiding earthly witnesses to bear the light of truth to places far and near. But in Greek, the original language of the New Testament, God refers to His earthly messengers by the same term used for heavenly angels—*angelos* (see Matt. 11:10; Luke 7:24; 9:52; 2 Cor. 8:23; James 2:25).[1] Those who accept the ever-advancing light of God's truth sound His words of warning and invitation to every part of the world.

The messages of Revelation's three angels burst forth at a time of great spiritual awakening in a world locked in the stifling grip of spurious religion and carnal illusions. A world that does not revere God or live for His glory or have any concept of personal accountability for the moral complexion of its life. A world that feels blithely and magnificently superior to "old-fashioned" Bible religion.

These messages will not be drowned out by the ridicule of human unbelief. The bearing of these messages earthward by angels represents the purity, urgency, and divine origin of the messages' content. With power and glory that none can ignore, the warning will accomplish a great work.

As we begin our consideration of the first angel's message, we should notice that these messages are God's final presentation of the everlasting gospel to the world. Unless we understand the gospel and remember that its light irradiates every facet of these messages, we will not be able to interpret them correctly or proclaim them in the right spirit. Some have treated the message of the three angels (Rev. 14:6-12) as a mandate to condemn people entangled in sin and error. What a grievous mistake! True, the gospel clears away the rubbish of error that humans and devils have erected as a barrier between heaven and earth. But this work of removing deception simply opens the way for *exalting the truth as it is in Jesus*. That is the unalterable nature of the gospel.

Romans 1:16, 17 explicitly defines the everlasting gospel. Paul declared, "The gospel of Christ . . . is the power of God to salvation for everyone who believes, for the Jew first and also for the Greek. For in it the righteousness of God is revealed from faith to faith; as it is written, 'The just shall live by faith.' "

From this passage we can see that:

1. The gospel is the supreme, all-sufficient manifestation of God's power to save us from sin.

2. This power is granted to all who believe.

3. The gospel reveals the righteousness of God (His perfect character of mercy and justice).

4. Anyone can receive Christ's righteousness by placing complete faith in Him and the saving merits of His sacrifice.

5. The beauty of the gospel is progressively revealed from one

level of faith to another. We cannot grasp the whole of its glory and power in one flash. But we are wholly accepted the instant we receive Christ as our Savior.

Calvary is the fountainhead of the gospel's irrepressible power. Paul declared Christ crucified to be the power and wisdom of God that silences all the arrogant philosophy of humankind (see 1 Cor. 1:17, 18, 23, 24).

But the cross is not an amulet or a magic wand. In itself it possesses no supernatural power and is not to be worshiped. Apart from Christ, the cross stands as an emblem of humanity's brutality, disgrace, and stark emptiness of spirit. But Christ crucified reverses our natural destiny, bringing forth the blessing of salvation where once existed only the curse of doom. God turned *our* supreme act of alienation from Him into *His* supreme act of reconciliation toward us. As we consider all that Christ endured to deliver us from our lost state, our hearts are transformed. Pressing closer to the Cross every day, we plead with God to awaken our hearts to the fullness of redeeming love displayed there. And joyfully will He disclose to us the exhaustless treasures of Calvary love, including its power to save us from sin and make us partakers of the divine nature. "The cross of Calvary, rightly regarded, is true philosophy, pure and undefiled religion. It is eternal life to all who believe."[2]

Countless streams of influence flow constantly from the Cross to cleanse us from our defilement and fill us with the fullness of God's grace and love if we are receptive to His work on our behalf. "One steadfast look at the Saviour uplifted on the cross will do more to purify the mind . . . than will all the scientific explanations by the ablest tongue."[3]

We can correctly understand Christ's atoning sacrifice only through a constant, prayerful study of the Scriptures. To form our own mystical impressions about Christ without a careful reading of the Word is to open ourselves to great delusion. Paul warmly commended the believers at Colossae for their wholehearted acceptance "of the word of the truth of the gospel, which has come to you as it has also in all the world, and is bringing forth fruit and growing . . .

since the day you heard it and knew the grace of God in truth" (Col. 1:5, 6). He warned the Colossians not to depart from the scriptural integrity of the gospel by assimilating ideas that subvert Scripture (see Col. 2:1-10).

In Galatians 1:6-9 Paul warned against perverted gospels that are no gospel at all, even though they may extol many of the general features of Christianity. God's final gospel invitation comes at a time when false gospels proliferate like competing commercial products. The aim of the first angel's message is exalt the true, everlasting gospel with fresh intensity and error-destroying effect. This accounts for the potent warning features of the message.

" 'Fear God' "

Like a flurry of royal trumpets, the first angel's message opens on an imperative chord: " 'Fear God!' " Godly fear is the antithesis of earthly fear and is the only effective safeguard against it. Human wisdom would suggest that the first angel's message should have begun with the soothing words "Trust God." Certainly, God does want us to trust Him. Anyone acquainted with Scripture realizes it would be a deplorably twisted conclusion to suppose that God wants us to live in terror of Him. The Bible reveals that throughout history God has encouraged the weak and insecure not to be afraid (evidenced by the many "fear not's" in Scripture).

God has no wish to frighten us, but He has a special reason for starting the first angel's message on so authoritative a note. Satan has deceived the modern world into taking God's Word lightly, as though it were a fable or mere compilation of ancient maxims and legends rather than a perfect revelation of truth. This disdainful attitude toward Scripture has caused people to lose their spiritual bearings and fall for every species of lie the devil can invent. Reverence for God and absolute belief in His sovereignty and the authority of His Word are well-nigh obliterated from the human mind. Divine truths are made the sport of entertainers and educators. All this degrades the human spirit and rushes the world on to ruin.

The command to fear God is an awakening call to trust and obey the supreme Authority of the universe. His law is not a jest. His decrees are not an option. His prophecies are not a guess. His promises are not a hoax. God's Word is inspired. It is spirit and life. It is eternal. It is living, powerful. It creates. It re-creates repentant sinners. It shields believers from sin. It sanctifies the heart. It is Heaven's guiding light. It is food to the soul and joy to those who believe and practice its teachings. It cannot be overthrown.

Paul declared that the wicked have "no fear of God before their eyes" (Rom. 3:18). They treat Him as a non-entity. Though they dismiss His Word as an irrelevance, they gladly receive human opinions that pander to carnality. However, when in their lost condition they face Christ in the judgment, they will stand aghast at their lazy indifference to the solid claims of truth, at their scorn for divine revelation, at their breezy, smirking unbelief. Then their terror will be boundless, their doom irreversible (Rev. 6:15-17; cp. 1 Pet. 3:12).

It is precisely to spare us from this experience that God enjoins us to regard Him now with "godly fear"—solemn reverence—which is a tonic to the soul. Such fear is the fruit of grace and is a blessed thing (see Heb. 12:28, 29). "In the fear of the Lord there is strong confidence, and His children will have a place of refuge. The fear of the Lord is a fountain of life to turn one away from the snares of death." "The fear of the Lord leads to life, and he who has it will abide in satisfaction; he will not be visited with evil." "Who is the man that fears the Lord? Him shall He teach in the way that He chooses." "The secret of the Lord is with those who fear Him, and He will show them His covenant." (Prov. 14:26, 27; 19:23; Ps. 25:12, 14.)

" 'Give glory to Him' "

Just as imperative and telegraphically intense as the injunction " 'Fear God' " is the angel's next command: " 'Give glory to Him' "! To give glory to God is to be savingly united with Christ and through that union to reveal His love to the world (2 Thess. 1:11, 12). It means self-crucifixion that Christ may be magnified in all the plans, activities, and relations of life (Phil. 1:20, 21). It means exhibiting not only freedom from sin but also the active virtues of God's love. "It is the glory of the gospel that it is founded upon the principle of restoring in the fallen race the divine image by a constant manifestation of benevolence."[4]

Christ wishes to manifest Himself and His Father through us. The more fully we unite with Him, the more abundantly do we give glory to Him by revealing His attributes (John 17:24; 1 Cor. 6:20, 21). A famous preacher visited a large church that was packed to capacity to hear his message. Just before the preacher arose to speak, an aged deacon offered this prayer: "Lord, we thank thee for Brother Jowett, who is about to address us. Now blot him out that the glory of Your Son alone may shine through his manner and message." When self is submerged in Christ and transformed into His likeness, we shall have a quickening influence on others to dispel darkness and attract them to the Savior. Thus, through the principle of spiritual reproduction, we bring forth fruit to His glory (see Gal. 5:22, 23; Eph. 5:8-10; John 4:35, 38; 12:24-26).

> Christ has made provision that His church shall be a transformed body, illumined with the light of heaven, possessing the glory of Immanuel. It is His purpose that every Christian shall be surrounded with a spiritual atmosphere of light and peace. There is no limit to the usefulness of the one, who, putting self aside, makes room for the working of the Holy Spirit upon his heart and lives a life wholly consecrated to God. . . .
>
> It is the privilege of every Christian, not only to look for, but to hasten the coming of our Lord Jesus Christ. Were all who profess His name bearing fruit to His glory, how quickly would the whole world be sown with the seed of the gospel. Quickly the last harvest would be ripened, and Christ would come to gather the precious grain.[5]

Christ said, " 'By this My Father is glorified, that you bear much fruit; so will you be My disciples.' " " 'You did not choose Me, but I chose you and appointed you that you should go and bear fruit, and that your fruit should remain.' " (John 15:8, 16). This is the fruit of everlasting righteousness begotten in willing hearts through the power of the everlasting gospel. Such fruit of character makes us productive in soul winning (see 1 Thess. 1:5-10).

" 'The hour of His judgment is come' "

The next phase of the first angel's message is the solemn proclamation " 'The hour of His judgment is come' " (Rev. 14:7). Christ's own words affirm the integral connection of the judgment with the gospel. As the gospel incarnate, He declared, " 'For judgment I am come into this world' " and " 'The Father has committed all judgment to the Son' " (John 9:39; 5:22, cp. 12:47-50). Christ conducts His judgment in the sanctuary above. Accordingly, the first angel's message directs us to Christ's ministration in the heavenly sanctuary as our Intercessor and Judge (see Revelation 1–5, Daniel 7, and the book of Hebrews).

Divine judgment clarifies issues, ends evildoing, rectifies wrongs, vindicates right, defends the harmless, punishes wrongdoers, and upholds the honorable. Judgment that is just is a majestic, noble thing that ensures the peace of all who love righteousness and guarantees spiritual health throughout the universe. "The Lord shall endure forever; He has prepared His throne for judgment. He shall judge the world in righteousness, and He shall administer judgment for the peoples in uprightness" (Ps. 9:7, 8; read the whole psalm).

> "The hour of His judgment is come," points to the closing work of Christ's ministration for the salvation of men. It heralds a truth which must be proclaimed until the Saviour's intercession shall cease, and He shall return to this earth to take His people to Himself.[6]

In Jesus, mercy and truth have met together, righteousness and peace have kissed each other in a permanent, invincible partnership sealed on Calvary, thus guaranteeing perfect love and justice in every phase of the judgment. We will take a closer look at this theme in chapter 10.

" 'Worship Him who made . . .' "

Humans worship instinctively. But our instincts, perverted since the entrance of sin, do not naturally lead us into a healthy, enlightened worship experience. The majority of earth's inhabitants worship idols. These idols are not just solid objects, literal images, but false concepts of God. Such worship is unholy (Rom. 1:20-28).

True worship is rooted in a clear, reverent awareness that God is our Creator and Sustainer. This fact is highlighted by the angel's command, " 'Worship Him who made heaven and earth, the sea and springs of water' " (Rev. 14:7). "The Lord is great, and greatly to be praised; He is to be feared above all gods. For all the gods of the peoples are idols, but the Lord made the heavens" (Ps. 96:4, 5). "You are worthy, O Lord, to receive glory and honor and power; for You created all things, and by Your will they exist and were created" (Rev. 4:11). We owe our existence to God. Nothing can change this fact, no future development can alter its fundamental importance. (See Isaiah 43–46 for an extensive development of this point.)

A clear-minded worship of our Creator leads to endlessly uplifting results in the life of the worshiper. Recognizing that we have been made in God's image (Gen. 1:26, 27; Matt. 19:4-6), we are delivered from the deep-rooted identity crisis that bedevils most modern people, the majority of whom have been taught that we are the offspring of biochemical happenstance without any Creator to give purpose, direction, or spiritual destiny to our lives. The knowledge that we are children of the heavenly King not only spares us from the comfortless implications of evolution, but also inspires us with a sense of life's intrinsic value and noble possibilities.

Those who worship God as their Creator will actively pursue all the light they can obtain from His Word on every dimension of life. They will enjoy believing and practicing God's counsel on every matter He addresses. They will study all that He has revealed about wholesome and true worship and renounce their own ideas about so sacred a matter. Their hearts will be inspired to "worship the Lord in the beauty of holiness" rather than to pursue self-glorification disguised as worship.

In Christ's day, the various factions of Judaism contended extensively about doctrine and forms of worship. Jesus declared that " 'true worshipers will worship the Father in spirit and truth; for the Father is seeking such to worship Him' " (John 4:23).

> Jesus had come to teach the meaning of the worship of God, and He could not sanction the mingling of human requirements with the divine precepts.
>
> The religion that comes from God is the only religion that will lead to God. In order to serve Him aright, we must be born of the divine Spirit. This will purify the heart and renew the mind, giving us a new capacity for knowing and loving God. *It will give us a willing obedience to all His requirements. This is true worship.* It is the fruit of the working of the Holy Spirit.[7]

David prayed, "Your hands have made me and fashioned me; give me understanding that I may learn Your commandments" (Ps. 119:73). Among these commandments is one that explicitly identifies the Lawgiver as the Creator. It is the fourth commandment, which designates the seventh-day Sabbath as the memorial of God's creation. The very wording of the first angel's message echoes this commandment, thus summoning the world to reform in a matter about which it has grown careless and forgetful (cp. Rev. 14:7; Exod. 20:11).

Historically, the first angel's message was first proclaimed in the early 1840s. Its proclamation has proceeded with steadily widening influence since then.

> The first angel's message of Revelation 14, announcing the hour of God's judgment, and calling upon men to fear and worship Him, was designed to separate the professed people of God from the corrupting influences of the world, and to arouse them to see their true condition of worldliness and backsliding. In this message God had sent to the church a warning, which, had it been accepted, would have corrected

> the evils that had been shutting them away from Him. Had they received the message from heaven, humbling their hearts before the Lord, and seeking in sincerity a preparation to stand in His presence, the Spirit and power of God would have been manifested among them. The church would again have reached that blessed state of unity, faith, and love, which existed in apostolic days, when the believers "were of one heart and of one soul," and "spake the word of God with boldness," when "the Lord added daily to the church such as should be saved."[8]

For all who accept it and walk in its light, this message is the glorious water of life that flows from the throne of God to cleanse, refresh, and heal the soul.

---

1. See also Ellen G. White, *The Great Controversy* (Nampa, Idaho: Pacific Press, 1950), 312.
2. White, *Sons and Daughters of God* (Hagerstown, Md.: Review and Herald, 1983), 231.
3. White, *Manuscript Releases* (Silver Spring, Md.: The E. G. White Estate, 1990), 4:121.
4. White, *Testimonies for the Church* (Nampa, Idaho: Pacific Press, 1948), 9:254.
5. Ibid., 8:19, 22.
6. *The Great Controversy*,435, 436.
7. White, *The Desire of Ages* (Nampa, Idaho: Pacific Press, 1940), 82, 189; emphasis supplied.
8. *The Great Controversy*, 379.

CHAPTER SIX

LOVE'S FINAL APPEAL

Rulers get a bird's-eye view of life. They have a panoramic survey of the world, a global perspective of the vast array of human behavior. Gifted to be the world's wisest man, King Solomon had exceptional advantages as an observer of life. His book Ecclesiastes—particularly the first two chapters—testifies that he circumnavigated the sphere of human passion and ambition, sorrow and satisfaction, failure and achievement. Under the inspiration of God's Spirit, Solomon distilled his observations into proverbs (see Eccles. 12:9-11) that have served as a guiding light to thinking people for half the world's history.

One of his proverbs, given twice in his collection, says, "The prudent man foresees evil and hides himself, but the simple pass on and are punished" (Prov. 22:3; 27:12). The prudent are not cowards who shrink from danger and duty. Rather, they see that their only safety and vantage ground for serving God in this rebellious world is to take constant refuge in Christ. They heed His warnings because they know that God's people do not live by bread alone but by every word that proceeds from the mouth of the Lord. Moreover, they recognize that God's truth is not a tentative hypothesis or a bendable proposition, but an authoritative revelation that calls for belief and obedience.

In Revelation 14:8-11 we read God's final warning and appeal to the human family, His last invitation of mercy. He sends His warnings no less than His invitations in a spirit of perfect love. A warning implies concern for the safety and well-being of others. And when God warns, then we can be sure that our response determines our destiny.

Following the first angel's call to pure worship of the Creator and the announcement that His investigative judgment has begun in preparation for Christ's return (Rev. 14:6, 7), the Lord cautions us regarding Satan's devices cunningly wrought to nullify the gospel. Through degrading our senses and confusing our judgment, Satan purposes to make evil look good and good seem evil. God's plan is to use the power of truth to extricate us from all confusion and moral contamination. Righteousness can have no fellowship with unrighteousness; and light, no communion with darkness.

Foreseeing the evil that would encompass the earth (see Isa. 60:1; 2 Tim. 3:1-5) and the corruptions that would infest the nominal Christian world, the Lord prepared a special message in Revelation for earth's final age. This message is given to restore eternal truth and expose the spiritual delusions that Satan casts abroad to ensnare and destroy the human family. Because many of these delusions are set forth in the name of the gospel, it is all the more imperative for God to expose these counterfeits. Nothing is more insidious or fatal than doctrines of demons that appear to be of heavenly origin but that are calculated to alienate us from truth and separate us from God. After all, it was through *false religious doctrine*, beguiling error, that Satan brought ruin to the human race through our first parents. He raised *spiritual topics,* presented from his point of view: life, death, obedience to God, and the authority of His Word.

Through error Satan caused our first parents to separate from God, and it is through truth that our connection with God is restored and maintained. Jesus said, " 'If you abide in My word, you are My disciples indeed, and you shall know the truth, and the truth shall make you free.' " He prayed to His Father, " 'Sanctify them by Your truth. Your word is truth' " (John 8:31, 32; 17:17).

However, it takes more than an articulation of sound doctrine to break the spell of error and restore sin-damaged lives to God. Christ came as the living embodiment of all truth. He is the way, the truth, and the life; no one comes to the Father but by Him (see John 14:6, 7). Faith in His atoning blood alone reclaims us from sin and opens the way for us to receive the truth as a living power. That is why God entitles His final plea to humanity the "everlasting gospel."

God denounces error simply to clear the way for the restoration of truth to its rightful position—that of supreme authority in the universe, fully displayed in its infinitely attractive character, content, and communicative openness. The three messages of Rev. 14:6-12 combined remove the obscuring veil of misperception concerning God's character and magnify Christ and His righteousness with climactic intensity.

The messages

Christ taught that adherence to religious traditions that conflict with divine revelation results in vain worship. It is precisely to counteract this fatally misleading influence that the Lord declares, " 'Babylon is fallen, is fallen, because she made all nations drink of the wine of the wrath of her fornication' " (Rev. 14:8).

Christ symbolized His new covenant by a cup filled with unfermented grape juice, typifying the cleansing, life-giving virtue of His blood. Babylon, which is apostate Christendom, dispenses the intoxicating wine of a counterfeit covenant. Its substitute replaces the Word of God with the traditions of men, mingling doctrines of demons with the glorious truths of Scripture—thereby offering up a mixture of confusion, of falsehoods parasitically intertwined with sacred verities. The Lord wants us to understand that His new covenant does not modify or abrogate the moral law or lower the standard of excellence in human character and conduct. Rather, the whole object of His covenant is to bring us into rich accord with the principles of His government. These principles are defined in the Decalogue and exemplified in Christ's person, in which human nature is linked with the divine through His voluntary dependence on the Father (see Matt. 5:17-19; 1 John 2:3-6; 5:3-5; Heb. 8:10-12).

Satan's reactional opposition to truth, mediated in large part through apostate Christian churches, necessitates the sounding of the third angel's message:

> A third angel followed them, saying with a loud voice, "If anyone worships the beast and his image, and receives his mark on his forehead or in his hand, he himself shall also drink of the wine of the wrath of God, which is poured out full strength into the cup of His indignation. And he shall be tormented with fire and brimstone in the presence of the holy angels and in the presence of the Lamb. And the smoke of their torment ascends forever and ever; and they have no rest day or night, who worship the beast and his image, and whoever receives the mark of his name." Here is the patience of the saints; here are those who keep the commandments of God and the faith of Jesus (Rev. 14:9-12).

The ostensible centerpiece of this message is a supercharged warning against the mark of the beast. Yet behind this alarm is a call to look beyond the turmoil of Satan's angry religion to the pure invitation of love streaming from the heart of God. " 'Look to Me and be saved, all you ends of the earth!' " He declares (Isa. 45:22). "I will never attempt to force your conscience, as Satan does through his religious system called Babylon. Rather, I invite you to receive My Son Jesus as your Savior and your righteousness." In exposing Satan's false religion, the Lord clears the way for His truth to shine forth without distortion or obscurity. That is what turns the negative features of this last message into a resoundingly positive force. It unmasks error only to redirect our attention to eternal, soul-saving truth.

Saturated with Christ's righteousness

To see how this message is truly saturated with a revelation of Christ's righteousness, let's analyze its components and their connection.

(1) Flying to this earth with swiftness and energy, the third angel warns against worshiping the beast and his image. This correlates with the first angel's message that enjoins us to worship God the Creator. In Scripture, the Lord repeatedly bases His claim to divinity on His power to create, direct, and sustain the entire universe (Jer. 51:15-19). This message warns us not to worship a created being who claims the right to be worshiped by acting as the final arbiter in matters of religious authority. Plainly, what is depicted here is not a conflict between religion versus non-religion, but between true and false religion. The issues at stake in that conflict spotlight the destiny-determining importance of knowing and worshiping the true God and of adhering without compromise to His Word (see John 17:3; 1 Cor. 1:10,11).

(2) The "beast" that demands human worship is introduced in Rev. 13:1-11. This passage symbolically portrays a persecuting religious power that incorporates features of extinct civilizations—Babylon, Persia, Greece, and Rome—that understood how to control the masses through pageantry, the occult, and hierarchical rule. This beast claims ancient roots of authority, and by its pomp and majesty commands the admiration of earthly powers. So nearly universal is the support it derives from world leaders that it feels emboldened to persecute God's saints—those who adhere to the law and testimony of God and refuse to submit to the false authority of tradition.

Satan unites the religions of the world through miracles. Then he lures this ecumenical alliance to establish a religious test for the entire population of the world. This test, a law bearing on worship, directly opposes the very command in God's law that enjoins us to worship Him as our Creator. That command is the Sabbath (Exod. 20:8-11), which sets apart the seventh day as holy in commemoration of God's having created this world in six days.

In defiant contrast, apostate Christian powers have substituted

Sunday as the appointed day of rest and worship. Rome's *magisterium ecclesia* justifies this change on the grounds of their church's supposed authority to change or modify divine law. Protestants advance Sunday keeping on other grounds: the pseudo-biblical assumption that Christ's death on Calvary abrogated or altered the Ten Commandments. This fallacy is far more insidious than Catholicism's candid acknowledgment that it ascribes higher authority to papal decrees and the tradition of the church than it does to Scripture. Sunday-keeping Protestantism, acting as a false prophet, uses Scripture to nullify God's own law—thus placing the Word at odds with itself.

The reasoning of these Protestants is the height of Babylonish confusion, the ultimate refinement of blasphemy, for "[God] has magnified [His] word above all [His] name" (Ps. 138:2). He will not break His covenant nor alter the word that has gone out of His lips. His word is forever settled in heaven. Answering the false charges against Him and foreseeing how Satan would seek to distort the gospel in future generations, Jesus declared that He did not come to destroy the law or the prophets but to fulfill them (Matt. 5:17-19; cp. Rom. 8:4; 1 John 2:3-5; 5:3). He insisted that it was easier for heaven and earth to pass away than for one tittle of God's law to fail (Luke 16:17). It is no wonder, then, that Scripture points to mandatory Sunday observance as the mark of the beast in contrast to God's sign and end-time seal—which, as we have already seen, is His Sabbath. Pointing to Christ as our Creator and Redeemer, the Sabbath of Scripture retains its gospel significance throughout eternal ages (see Mark 2:27, 28; Heb. 4).

(3) God answers Babylon's challenge to the world by raising up a body of Christians who worship Him in spirit and in truth. He identifies this people as those who keep the commandments of God and have the faith of Jesus (Rev. 14:12). No iron-fisted union of church and state, no spectacular display of demonically generated miracles, no degree of mystical and organizational unity among earth's deluded masses, no array of religious and political leaders pleading for submission to the Sunday law, can avail to lure the faithful remnant from their loyalty to Christ, who plainly states, " 'If you love Me, keep My commandments' " (John 14:15).

About those who formulate an adulterated version of Christianity to suit their own convenience, Jesus quoted the words of Isaiah, " ' "This people honors Me with their lips, but their heart is far from Me. And in vain they worship Me, teaching as doctrines the commandments of men." For laying aside the commandment of God, you hold the tradition of men' " (Mark 7:6-8). It is impossible for the rejecters of God's law to refute this solemn indictment. No amount of talk about divine love and grace can overthrow the eternal truth that God's law is immutable and that His grace is sufficient to bring our lives into harmony with both the spirit and the letter of the law. The gospel releases us from the penalty and power of sin, not from the blessing of obedience to God's law.

God's people demonstrate unflinching loyalty against a nearly overwhelming tide of opposition because they are maturely and securely anchored in Christ. His perfect love in their lives dispels all ungodly fear. Theirs is the experience of righteousness by faith lived out in the face of unprecedented hostility to God's purposes.

(4) Finally, God warns humanity not to provoke His wrath by defiance of the truth and persecution of those who faithfully obey His Word. God's wrath is an agonizing demonstration of His love. Divine love upholds righteousness and truth; it does not smile upon rebellious disobedience and violent intolerance. "The wrath of God is revealed from heaven against all ungodliness and unrighteousness of men, who suppress the truth in unrighteousness, because what may be known of God is manifest in them, for God has shown it to them" (Rom. 1:18, 19). The proponents of the mark of the beast have a deep-rooted animosity toward the Creator and consequently are hostile to those who signalize their loyalty to Him by keeping the weekly day of worship that commemorates His creative work.

> But not one is made to suffer the wrath of God until the truth is brought home to his mind and conscience, and has been rejected. There are many who have not had opportunity to hear the special truths for this time. The obligation of the fourth commandment has never been set before them in its

true light. He who reads every heart and tries every motive will leave none who desire a knowledge of the truth, to be deceived as to the issues of the controversy. The decree is not to be urged upon people blindly. Everyone is to have sufficient light to make his decision intelligently.[1]

Wrath, reluctantly manifested

God's wrath is the manifestation of His retributive justice, visited with infinite reluctance on those resolved to destroy His government of peace. His graphic description of the effect of His wrath arises from the depths of His knowing what Christ endured for us on Calvary to absorb the penalty of the violated law. In effect, the third angel's message pleads with people not to reject divine mercy and defiantly swallow the cup of judgment Christ drank in our place. Through His vivid description of the horrors of the second death in Revelation 14:10, 11, the Lord's voice resounds in clarion tones of urgent appeal from the very height of Golgotha. "Please do not drink from this cup of unutterable grief and abandonment," He says, "for I have drunk it for you. I offer in its stead the cup of salvation and joyous communion with Myself."

God does not want us to die in our sins. He makes every legitimate effort to pull sinners back from the abyss of ruin toward which they so boldly stride as though they were above reproach and beyond the reach of destruction. This last heaven-sent message of warning and appeal holds back nothing in its call for repentance toward God and faith toward our Lord Jesus Christ.

The message clearly identifies the options set before every person: obey God by His grace and receive His seal, or submit to Satan's power exerted through corrupt religious authorities and receive the mark of the beast.[2] Emphasizing, as they do, humanity's freedom of choice, God's final messages to the world magnify the principle of religious liberty as a cardinal feature of the divine government. "For where the Spirit of the Lord is, there is liberty." Christ and His truth make us free. Error and disobedience to God have no sanctifying properties, but cause alienation, degradation, and death—a fate that He wishes none to undergo.

> While you hold the banner of truth firmly, proclaiming the law of God, let every soul remember that the faith of Jesus is connected with the commandments of God. The third angel is represented as flying through the midst of heaven, crying with a loud voice, "Here are they that keep the commandments of God, and the faith of Jesus" (Rev. 14:12). The first, second, and third angels' messages are all linked together. The evidences of the abiding, ever-living truth of these grand messages, that mean so much to us, that have awakened such intense opposition from the religious world, cannot be extinguished. Satan is constantly seeking to cast his hellish shadow about these messages, so that the remnant people of God shall not clearly discern their import, their time, and place; but they live, and are to exert their power upon our religious experience while time shall last.
>
> The influence of these messages has been deepening and widening, setting in motion the springs of action in thousands of hearts, bringing into existence institutions of learning, publishing houses, and health institutions; all these are the instrumentalities of God to cooperate in the grand work represented by the first, second, and third angels flying in the midst of heaven to warn the inhabitants of the world that Christ is coming again with power and great glory.[3]

God identifies those who join with Him in proclaiming His final warning that exalts rejected truth and exposes popular error as repairers of the breach, restorers of streets to dwell in (see Isa. 58:12). Through His consecrated people shines the beauty of holiness, the joy of obedience, which is perfect harmony with the will of God. Under the inspiration of God's Spirit and the authority of His Word, they lighten the earth with the glory of the everlasting gospel (Rev. 18:1).

In response to this message, every true-hearted worshiper of God will come out of Babylon to join His commandment-keeping remnant (Rev. 18:1-5). Those who reject the message will confederate under earth's highest religio-political authorities to destroy the obedient children of God. This campaign of destruction will decree death for those who reject the mark of the beast. Such rabid intolerance will arouse the interest and conscience of all humanity. Many, previously uninterested in religious controversies and questions of divine law, will examine the issues in order to make a properly informed decision.

The two contrasting reactions to the message bring the world to its ultimate crisis of decision. Those who reject God's warning message in preference for the delusions that appeal to their carnal nature will be lost. And those who choose for Christ and His truth will triumph gloriously over the concerted hostility of human beings and devils, just as Israel did when crossing the Red Sea. Glorified at Christ's second coming, the faithful ascend to heaven, where they will sing the song of Moses, the servant of God, and the song of the Lamb. Theirs is an experience of loving obedience to divine law through the abundantly enabling grace of Christ slain for the salvation of humanity, the vindication of divine truth, and the final overthrow of all evil.

On a celestial chord of swelling power that magnifies Christ and His righteousness, the third angel's message closes with serene, triumphant finality: " 'Here is the patience of the saints, here are those who keep the commandments of God and the faith of Jesus' " (Rev. 14:12). The powers of evil can never prevent the fulfillment of this promise to the weakest saint who trusts and obeys the Lord by His grace.

---

1. Ellen G. White, *The Great Controversy* (Nampa, Idaho: Pacific Press, 1950), 605.

2. This destiny-determining choice and its spiritual implications are elucidated in such passages as Romans 6:15-23 and Deuteronomy 30:11-20. Both these passages are saturated with rich gospel encouragement for us all to make the right choice.

3. White, *Selected Messages* (Hagerstown, Md.: Review and Herald, 1958), 2:117, 118.

CHAPTER SEVEN

A LOVE STRONGER THAN DEATH

Early in the summer of 1822, the 30-year-old lyric poet Shelley was absorbed in writing a philosophical ode at his villa in Italy. One afternoon he broke from his task after penning the line " 'Then what is life,' I cried?" His question hovered on the page, begging to be answered. The next day, Shelley drowned in the Gulf of Spezia amid a violent storm that arose while he was boating with two friends. No one knows what Shelley intended to write in answer to his highly charged question, for he left no notes behind to indicate his thoughts on the subject.[1]

God's unfailing Word holds the answer to this query that commands the interest of all thinking people. Let us begin by looking at the origin of human life. Scripture reveals that God created human beings in His own image, "male and female He created them" (Gen. 1:27). God created this universe not in fumbling experimentation, but with power, wisdom, and understanding (Jer. 51:15). His creation of sensate beings and delicately interdependent life-systems, with their exquisitely designed form and function, displays not only infinite intelligence, but also the expressive and fellowship-seeking attributes of His love. He made us like Himself, in order that we may have endlessly satisfying fellowship with Him—fellowship infused with creative power and relational depth (see Isa. 43:7, 21; Eph. 1:3-5; 1 John 1:1-3).

By giving Adam and Eve reproductive powers, God shared with us His capacity to bring forth new life and lovingly care for its development. What a privilege! Powerful as the holy angels are, they do not possess this ability (Matt. 22:30). As a means of education and enjoyment, God gave Adam and Eve the pleasant work of tending Eden, their graceful garden home. As they became increasingly acquainted with the order, variety, and beauty of the Garden and of the cosmos beyond, these discoveries "filled their hearts with deeper love, and brought forth from their lips expressions of gratitude and reverence to their Creator."[2]

Adam and Eve did not possess unconditional immortality. They needed to eat fruit from the tree of life as a perpetual reminder that they owed their existence and its preservation to the loving Creator (see Ps. 100:3; John 15:4-6). They and their descendants were to remain ever mindful of this fundamental truth. We are not self-existent beings who can live apart from God and His specified conditions for the continuance of our lives.[3]

God created another tree destined to have a vital role in cosmic affairs—the tree of the knowledge of good and evil. He cautioned Adam and Eve not to eat of this tree, but placed it in the Garden as a test of their loyalty and obedience. It is integral to God's plan to allow all of His created intelligences freedom of choice. He seeks to guide us into exercising that freedom in loyal obedience to Him. But that obedience, to be authentic and mutually satisfying, must flow from a heart of willing love and well-informed judgment. Freedom of choice is at the root of all personal identity. Without this freedom we would be mere biological automatons (see Deut. 30:15, 16, 19, 20).

God did not create the tree of the knowledge of good and evil to tempt or trick anyone. He did it in response to a stupendously agonizing challenge. When God created this world, Satan had already rebelled against the divine government and chosen the pathway that leads to death. In His absolute integrity, God revealed to Adam and Eve the existence of the two conflicting systems of government, the two modes of life—righteousness, truth, and love versus evil, error, and hate.

Satan's lie about death

To prevent Adam and Eve's being caught off guard, the Lord informed them that the great adversary could have access to them only at the forbidden tree. Unfortunately, Eve made herself vulnerable by wandering over to that tree and gazing curiously at it. Genesis 3:1-7 concisely narrates Eve's ruinous encounter with Satan that day. As you review the familiar story of his fatal work of deception in Eden, consider his strategy and how successfully he continues to use it in multiple ways.

Satan did not reveal himself directly. Instead, he worked through an attractive and intelligent creature to beguile Eve. In his opening words to Eve, Satan asked a question—one that dripped with doubt and irony: "Yea, has God said. . . ?" In other words, "Who is this God, if he really is God? Is his word reliable? You have life independent of the so-called Creator. You are naturally immortal—a god whose true identity is being concealed from you so that you will live in subjection to someone who says he's your creator. How do you know you were created, and haven't always existed in some other state? You need only one more ingredient to make your happiness complete—Evil! This supernatural force will liberate all your dormant powers, make you able to think and act for yourself, and free you from this 'God's' domination. I've already proved him a liar by eating of the fruit in your presence, and I'm not dead. Here, try some; it will do you a world of good. Discover the goddess within, and embark on a new age of liberated living!"

Eve capitulated to this beguiling line of sophistry, the fatal effects of which Satan well knew. Then she drew her husband into this rebellion against the divine counsel. As a result, Satan's lies in Eden now permeate modern concepts of life both within and outside Christian cultures.

In propounding the lie that we are naturally immortal, Satan had a truly chilling and insidious long-range plan. By deceiving people into thinking that they are naturally immortal, he has been able to lure many into feeling absolutely independent of God because they assume that they are indestructibly self-existent. They expect that at death they will immediately ascend to a more exalted realm. This blunts their sense of accountability to God and throws open the door for attempting to establish communication with the enlightened "spirits" of those who have physically died and "graduated to" the next plane of existence. If people live on in a spirit world after death, it might seem reasonable to try to establish communication with them for guidance, comfort, and fellowship. But those "spirits" of the "departed" are merely fallen angels standing by to perpetuate Satan's first lie and thereby deepen humanity's alienation from God and intensify their degradation of character (see Isa. 8:19, 20; 1 Sam. 28:7-12; 1 Chron. 10:13, 14). When spirit mediums commune with the "dead," it is only demons with whom they are conversing (see Deut. 32:17; cp. Ps. 106:28; 1 Cor. 10:20; Rev. 13:13, 14; 16:13, 14).[4] That is why God's Word strictly forbids all attempted communication with the dead (see Deut. 18:10-13; Lev. 19:31).

Indeed, Scripture plainly teaches that the wages of sin is death, not advancement to some higher form of existence or consciousness (see Ezek. 18:20; Rom. 6:23). It says that the dead are powerless to think, feel, or communicate (see Job 14:12; Eccles. 9:5, 6, 10; Pss. 6:5; 115:17; 146:4) and that death is an unconscious sleep that continues until the resurrection at the end of time (see 1 Cor. 15:22, 23). Jesus referred to death as a sleep (see John 11:11-14), as did all the writers of Scripture who spoke of this subject (see, e.g., 1 Kings 2:10; 11:43; Acts 2:29, 34; 13:36, 37). Our only safeguard against spiritualism is the sure knowledge that God's Word speaks truly when it declares that "the dead know nothing" (Eccles. 9:5).

Modern men speak

Down through the ages, many consecrated ministers, theologians, and philosophers have propounded this basic understanding of the condition of souls in death—for example, Barnabas, Hermas, Polycarp, Ignatius, John Tyndale (Bible translator), John Locke, John Tillotson (seventeenth-century Archbishop of Canterbury), John Milton, Isaac Watts, Joseph Priestly, J. Olof Culberg, Harold Guillebaud (twentieth-century translator of the Bible into African languages), William Temple (twentieth-century Archbishop of Canterbury), James Moffatt (Bible translator), Reinhold Niebuhr, Karl Heim, Karl Barth, and John F. Taylor (principal of Wycliffe College).[5]

> The theory of the immortality of the soul was one of those false doctrines that Rome, borrowing from paganism, incorporated into the religion of Christendom. Martin Luther classed it with the "monstrous fables that form part of the Roman dunghill of decretals." Commenting on the words of Solomon in Ecclesiastes that the dead know not anything, the Reformer says: "Another place proving that the dead have no . . . feeling. There is, saith he, no duty, no science, no knowledge, no wisdom there. Solomon judgeth that the dead are asleep, and feel nothing at all. For the dead lie there, accounting neither days nor years, but when they are awaked, they shall seem to have slept scarce one minute."[6]

God alone inherently possesses immortality (see 1 Tim. 6:16). Nowhere does the Bible use the phrase "man's immortal soul." God is the Author and Sustainer of life; no being lives independently of Him. Christians are described as *seeking* immortality (see Rom. 2:7, cp. Job 4:17), a clear indication that they do not possess it innately. Immortality is a gift of God, not a law of nature or an inherent right. Failure to recognize this obliterates the truth that immortality is purchased for us through the sacrificial death of Christ and ratified by His resurrection. "Our Savior Jesus Christ . . . has abolished death and brought life and immortality to light through the gospel" (2 Tim. 1:10).

It is important to recognize that immediately upon accepting Jesus we receive the gift of eternal life. For the believer it is a present possession, not a delayed benefit (see John 5:24; 1 John 5:11-13; Rom. 6:23). Christ is the fountainhead of eternal life. He is the gospel personified. We obtain eternal life by receiving Christ's life and character attributes. These matchless blessings are not a reward but purely a gift of love granted to all who yield to God's saving grace and sovereign will. Eternal life consists in knowing Christ as one's personal Savior (John 17:2, 3). This knowledge is not just theoretical or doctrinal, but an actual merging of our minds and wills with God's. The glory of eternal life is not primarily in its duration, but in its being filled with the eternal presence and fellowship of God.

Christ made it clear, however, that those who possess eternal life in Him are still subject to the soul-sleep of death. He said to Martha, " 'I am the resurrection and the life. He who believes in Me, though he may die, he *shall* live' " (John 11:25, emphasis supplied). Jesus did not say, "Though he may die, he *still* lives." He declared that in the *future* He will bring forth from the grave those who die in Him (see John 5:28, 29). The resurrection of Lazarus is a type of the general resurrection that shall occur at Christ's second coming (see John 6:39, 40, 44; 1 Cor. 15:22, 23, 51-55; 1 Thess. 4:14-17).

The redeemed receive the gift of immortality at the time of Christ's second coming. They will then be raised in glorified bodies that are immune to sickness, aging, and fatigue—to deterioration of any kind. The redeemed will then be both physically and spiritually glorified. In this perfect state they will have eternal life—the Christ life within—*and* immortality—deathlessness in an incorruptible body like Christ's (see Phil. 3:20, 21).

The second choice

What, then, is the fate of those who reject the gift of eternal life offered through faith in Christ? All who reject the offer will perish. John 3:16, the most famous verse of the Bible, records Jesus' contrast of the two destinies between which we must all choose: eternal life through faith in Him or *extinction*. The original Greek word for "perish" in this verse, *appolumi*, means complete destruction, a vanishing into nothingness—not endless torments in fire, ice, or any other medium (see Ps. 37:10, 20, 38; Mal. 4:1-3; Matt. 15:13).

Christ distinguished between two resurrections: that which is to life and that which is to condemnation (see John 5:29; cp. Luke 14:14). At the end of the millennium, the Lord will come back to earth with His saints to visit judgment upon the rejecters of His truth and salvation. At that time, the lost will be resurrected *en masse* (see Rev. 20:5-9).[7] No sooner do they return to life than their anger and rebellion flare up anew. Even the unveiled revelation of God's glory does not move their hearts to repentance or righteousness (see Isa. 26:10; Rev. 20:7-9). They are as firmly entrenched in opposition to God as Satan himself. So, it is in mercy to them that God expunges them from their bitter, turbulent existence (see Prov. 8:36; Isa. 57:20, 21). Satan himself will be reduced to ashes (see Ezek. 28:17-19; Obad. 16; Jude 7; 2 Pet. 2:6).

In 1943 the archbishops of Canterbury and York commissioned fifty Anglican scholars and theologians to draft a joint statement on the progress of the gospel and the present duty of the church. Their resulting document contains an article that reads:

> Ultimately, all that is valueless in God's sight must and will be abolished, that . . . "God may be all and in all." Revelation and reason alike point to this ultimate consummation. The idea of the inherent indestructibility of the human soul (or consciousness) owes its origin to Greek, not to Bible, sources. The central theme of the New Testament is eternal life, not for everybody and anybody, but for believers in Christ as risen from the dead. The choice is set before man here and now. [God's] judgment may not at first sight appear to be "good news," yet it is integral to the gospel. It is the full assertion of the final triumph of good and the abolition of evil.[8]

We cannot leave this subject without carefully considering the infinite patience, mercy, and yearning love of God toward all, including those who most adamantly refuse His salvation. He "is not willing that any should perish, but that all should come to repentance." "God our Savior . . . desires all men to be saved and to come to the knowledge of the truth." (2 Pet. 3:9; 1 Tim. 2:4). Let us resolve by God's grace to be among those whom He will joyously welcome into His kingdom as ransomed, restored, and reunited followers of the Lamb and not have to hear His mournful words: " ' "I never knew you; depart from Me, you who practice lawlessness!" ' " (Matt. 7:23).

The waters of salvation flow freely over all the world. God longs to extend peace to us like a river. He longs to rejoice over us with singing. Meanwhile, His voice of invitation goes forth with tender entreaty: " 'Look to Me, and be saved, all you ends of the earth! For I am God, and there is no other' " (Isa. 45:22). May we respond with wholehearted willingness and desire, for the invitation comes from One who, at infinite expense to Himself, has abolished death and brought life and immortality to light through the gospel.

---

1. Judging from the tenor of the poem and his other writings, Shelley's views on this subject were mystical, subjective, and completely unbiblical.

2. Ellen G. White, *The Spirit of Prophecy* (Hagerstown, Md.: Review and Herald, 1969), 1:27.

3. See White, *Patriarchs and Prophets* (Hagerstown, Md.: Review and Herald, 1958), 52-55.

4. See also White, *The Great Controversy* (Nampa, Idaho: Pacific Press, 1950), 551-554.

5. See LeRoy Edwin Froom's *The Conditionalist Faith of Our Fathers*, (Hagerstown, Md.: Review and Herald, 1965). This exhaustive two-volume study on the nature and destiny of humankind stands without a rival in its field historically as well as theologically.

6. *The Great Controversy*, 549.

7. Ibid., 662-673.

8. *Towards the Conversion of England*, Section 53; cited in *The Conditionalist Faith of Our Fathers*, 2:818.

CHAPTER EIGHT

THE ETERNAL GOD IS YOUR REFUGE

Charles Wesley sat by an open window one day contemplating the landscape. A hawk suddenly flashed into view, rapidly gaining on a little bird. Sighting but one avenue of escape, the bird darted through the open window and in its confusion landed on Wesley, hiding behind the flap of his coat. With an angry screech, the hawk wheeled away.

Wesley quickly saw the parallel between this touching incident and the Lord's sheltering care for His people as they flee life's threats. Some have supposed that this incident gave rise to Wesley's hymn:

Jesus, lover of my soul,
Let me to Thy bosom fly,
While the billows near me roll,
While the tempest still is high.
Hide me, O my Saviour hide,
Till the storm of life is past;
Safe into the haven guide,
O, receive my soul at last.

Such longing for God's protection and care is deeply embedded in the hearts of all God's children. David cried out, "Oh that I had wings like a dove! for then would I fly away, and be at rest. . . . I would hasten my escape from the windy storm and tempest" (Ps. 55:6, 8, KJV). It was to provide spiritual refuge from sin and a place for inward restoration that God established His sanctuary for the children of Israel.

The very word *sanctuary* implies an unassailable, hallowed place of refuge. We think of bird sanctuaries, for instance, as places specially dedicated to protect birds from hunters and predators. Likewise, God established His sanctuary in Israel for the spiritual protection, purification, guidance, and refreshment of His people. The Hebrew word for sanctuary (*miqdosh*) means "a consecrated place, sanctuary, or asylum." In the verb form, its root (*qadosh*) means to cleanse, purify, and consecrate. The noun form of this root (*qodesh*) signifies a place where sanctification, purification, or cleansing occurs.

It is God's purpose not only to give us deliverance from oppression and refuge from outward danger, but also protection and purification from sin. Thus we are free to have fellowship with Him that we "might serve Him without fear, in holiness and righteousness before Him all the days of our life" (Luke 1:74, 75).

Origin and purpose of the sanctuary

After delivering the children of Israel from bondage to Egypt, the Lord demonstrated His care for their needs by providing them water in the desert where no water had been and manna from heaven. He also gave them His law, which reveals His unchanging moral character. Then God gave Moses instructions for the building of His sanctuary. He declared, " 'Let them make Me a sanctuary, that I may dwell among them' " (Exod. 25:8). What a loving purpose! He will ultimately achieve it by tabernacling with us in the new earth (see Rev. 21:3).

Everything that the Lord taught Israel through His earthly sanctuary was designed to prepare them for fully restored fellowship in future glory. It revealed to them the source of power for godly living in this present world. In the design of His sanctuary and its services, nothing was superfluous, nothing was left to the imagination of Moses and his helpers (see Exod. 25:40). Just so, in the plan of salvation, nothing is left to human devising or conjecture. Not only did God impart to Moses the exact plan for the construction and materials of the sanctuary, He also gave skill to those appointed to carry out the plan and provided the necessary materials. Thus, He always gives us the ability to carry out His appointed will if we choose to live in harmony with His ways.

God directed that His portable tabernacle in the wilderness be situated in the center of Israel's encampment. Their tents were to surround the sanctuary in an orderly arrangement, and their home life was to be a fragrant extension of all the lessons taught in that center appointed for holy worship. Accordingly, their tents and encampment were to be clean, as were their bodies, clothing, food, habits, and language. And through the righteousness of God, their minds and hearts were also to be clean (Pss. 24:3, 4; 73:1).

Every Israelite was to regard as paramount the call of "holiness to the Lord" through the cleansing blood of the divine Sacrifice, typified by the lambs, goats, and bullocks sacrificed at the altar in the tabernacle. Thus, true worship of God was to pervade their lives. Every phase and feature of the sanctuary service pointed to God as the ultimate sanctuary for His people (see Isa. 8:14; Ezek. 11:16; Jer. 17:12).

Every implement, every article of furniture in the sanctuary, every ritual performed, and every priestly garment worn was to be refulgent with the beauty of holiness. "In His temple everything saith, Glory" (Ps. 29:9, KJV, margin). There God's visible presence, the Skekinah, shone forth with as much brightness as mortal sight could endure. God's aim was to teach His people to walk in the light of Christ's fellowship and word. The work of the priests, the character of the feasts, the nature of the daily sacrifices, the type and quality of the provisions—all were imbued with gospel lessons. All that comprised the sanctuary and its services richly expressed the central truth of righteousness by faith in the atoning Sacrifice (see Lev. 17:11, cp. Rom. 3:24-26).

The morning and evening sacrifices (Exod. 29:38-46) were the foundation of the sanctuary services, pointing to Christ our Passover, sacrificed for us. They taught how the broken connection between human beings and God can be restored. Sin separates humans from their Creator (see Isa. 59:2). Those who accept Christ's sacrifice have their hearts transmuted into God's sacred abode. "Thus says the High and Lofty One who inhabits eternity, whose name is Holy: 'I dwell in the high and holy place, with him who has a contrite and humble spirit, to revive the spirit of humble, and to revive the heart of the contrite ones' " (Isa. 57:15).

With these great gospel verities shining forth from God's appointed system and place of worship, it is no wonder that the psalmist declares, "Thy way, O God, is in the sanctuary; who is so great a God as our God?" "They have seen thy goings O God; even the goings of my God, my King, in the sanctuary." "To see Thy power and Thy glory, so as I have seen Thee in the sanctuary. Because Thy lovingkindness is better than life, my lips shall praise Thee." (Pss. 77:13; 68:24; 63:2, 3, KJV.)

What the sanctuary represented

Through the symbolic merits of the blood of the sacrifices, the priests entered the sanctuary and represented the prayers and needs of the people at the golden altar of incense. This altar stood before the veil that separated the two apartments of the sanctuary—the Holy and Most Holy Places. Behind the veil was the ark of God's testament. This beautiful chest overlaid with gold was flanked by two golden cherubim, which signified the intimate participation of the angels in guiding people to the Savior and revealing to them His glorious way. Upon the ark was the crowned mercy seat, signifying Christ and His righteousness provided both as a substitute and example for humanity and proving wholly efficacious to all who in faith accept the merits of His atonement. Beneath the mercy seat were the tablets containing the Ten Commandments, which God Himself wrote with His own finger. Christ and His righteousness stand between us and the divine law, which we all have violated. If we do not frustrate Christ's grace but welcome Him, He will bring us into full harmony with the requirements of His law (see Rom. 8:4; 1 John 2:2-6; 5:3, 4). That is why He can be just and the Justifier of all who believe. His sacrificial death forgives us. His holy life credited to our blemished life record and implanted within us constitutes our righteousness. Thus, "if any man be in Christ, He is a new creation. Old things are passed away, behold all things are become new" (2 Cor. 5:17).

The Lord met with Moses at the mercy seat to reveal to him wondrous things for the enlightenment of His people (see Exod. 25:22). And He met with His people at the door of the tabernacle. His revelations concerning His will showed them how to live as holy temples for His habitation (see 1 Cor. 6:19, 20).

God prescribed animal sacrifices to symbolize the gospel teaching that we are saved only by the merits of Christ's blood applied. The Lord did not thirst for these sacrifices. They were not for His gratification or appeasement, but for the people's instruction. He did not delight in the blood or in the suffering of the animals whose lives were yielded to awaken people to the high cost of sin and the Redeemer's expiatory love. Through Hosea He declared, " 'I desire mercy and not sacrifice, and the knowledge of God more than burnt offerings' " (Hos. 6:6, cp. Ps. 40:6). "Will the Lord be pleased with thousands of rams or ten thousand rivers of oil? . . . He has shown you, O man, what is good; and what does the Lord require of you but to do justly, to love mercy, and to walk humbly with your God?" (Mic. 6:7, 8; cp. Deut. 5:29). "The sacrifices of God are a broken spirit; a broken and a contrite heart—These,O God, You will not despise" (Ps. 51:17).

God's aim was not to teach ritualism but to reveal righteousness through the symbolic services of the sanctuary. Wishing to convey the lesson that His righteousness is a divine, blood-bought gift of love, God directed Moses at Sinai to sprinkle the people, the book of the law, the tabernacle, and all the vessels of the ministry with blood. By this ceremony He ratified His covenant of redemption with Israel and emphasized that obedience to the divine requirements is possible only through the saving merits of His sacrifice (see Exod. 24:4-8; Heb. 9:19-21).

However, through carnality and love of the world, the Israelites did not retain the gospel lessons embodied in their religious services. They boasted of the temple and its services and performed its rituals with pagan gusto and obtuseness. But they were largely heedless of the lessons taught therein. It was all a work of the flesh rather than a humble demonstration of repentance and faith. Substituting their religion for the knowledge of God, they sank into spiritual insensibility and wicked living—all the while maintaining the outward forms of piety (see Jer. 7:1-11, 23, 24). The spirit in which they took the lives of the animals appointed for sacrifice was an ironic prophecy of what their descendants would do to Christ (see Isa. 1:11-20).

> As they departed from God, the Jews in a great degree lost sight of the teaching of the ritual service. That service had been instituted by Christ Himself. In every part it was a symbol of Him; and it had been full of vitality and spiritual beauty. But the Jews lost the spiritual life from their ceremonies, and clung to the dead forms. They trusted to the sacrifices and ordinances themselves, instead of resting upon Him to whom they pointed. In order to supply the place of that which they had lost, the priests and rabbis multiplied requirements of their own; and the more rigid they grew, the less of the love of God was manifested. They measured their holiness by the multitude of their ceremonies, while their hearts were filled with pride and hypocrisy.[1]
>
> Christ was the foundation and life of the temple. Its services were typical of the sacrifice of the Son of God. The priesthood was established to represent the mediatorial character and work of Christ. The entire plan of sacrificial worship was a foreshadowing of the Saviour's death to redeem the world. There would be no efficacy in these offerings when

the great event toward which they had pointed for ages was consummated.

Since the whole ritual economy was symbolical of Christ, it had no value apart from Him. When the Jews sealed their rejection of Christ by delivering Him to death, they rejected all that gave significance to the temple and its services. Its sacredness had departed. It was doomed to destruction. From that day, sacrificial offerings and the service connected with them were meaningless. Like the offering of Cain, they did not express faith in the Saviour. In putting Christ to death, the Jews virtually destroyed their temple. When Christ was crucified, the inner veil of the temple was rent in twain from top to bottom, signifying that the great final sacrifice had been made, and that the system of sacrificial offerings was forever at an end.[2]

Christ supersedes the sanctuary

Gabriel had told Daniel that Christ would supersede and end the sacrificial system by His death and subsequent inauguration as our heavenly high priest: " 'Messiah shall be cut off, but not for Himself . . . Then shall He confirm the covenant with many for one week; but in the middle of the week, He shall bring an end to sacrifice and offering' " (Dan. 9:26, 27, cp. Isa. 53:10-12). When Christ died on Calvary, He declared, "It is finished." At that precise moment the temple veil was torn in two from top to bottom, signifying that the ritual service was no longer needed because the divine Reality had met the symbolic type.

Christ's words did not signify that His work was finished, that nothing else must be done to bring the plan of salvation into full effect. But they did mean that His sacrifice was sufficient. Drinking His proffered cup of salvation, we call on the name of the Lord who has dealt so bountifully with us and exercise faith in His promise to complete the good work He has begun in our lives. It is the Father's purpose that Christ may dwell in our hearts by faith, that we "being rooted and grounded in love, . . . might be filled with all the fullness of God" (Eph. 3:16, 19).

The Jewish tabernacle was a type of the Christian church. . . .

The church on earth, composed of those who are faithful and loyal to God, is the "true tabernacle," whereof the Redeemer is the minister. God, and not man, pitched this tabernacle on a high, elevated platform. This tabernacle is Christ's body, and from north, south, east, and west, He gathers those who shall help to compose it.

Through Christ the true believers are represented as being built together for an habitation of God through the Spirit. Paul writes: "God, who is rich in mercy, for His great love wherewith He loved us, even when we were dead in sins, hath quickened us together with Christ, . . . and hath raised us up together, and made us sit together in heavenly places in Christ Jesus; that in the ages to come He might show the exceeding riches of His grace in His kindness toward us through Christ Jesus. For by grace are ye saved through faith; and that not of yourselves; it is the gift of God; not of works, lest any man should boast. For we are His workmanship, created in Christ Jesus unto good works, which God hath before ordained that we should walk in them. . . . Ye are no more strangers and foreigners, but fellow-citizens with the saints, and of the household of God; and are built upon the foundation of the apostles and prophets, Jesus Christ Himself being the chief corner-stone; in whom all the building fitly framed together groweth unto a holy temple in the Lord; in whom ye also are builded together for a habitation of God through the Spirit."

God employed men to rear the Jewish tabernacle, giving them skill and efficiency for their work. [See Ex. 35:30–36:4.] . . . Thus heavenly intelligences cooperated with the workmen whom God Himself selected. And thus the church on earth must unite with the heavenly intelligences in doing God's work for this time. . . .

Men and women will not be saved unless they themselves exercise faith, and build on the true foundation, unless they

> allow God to recreate them by His Holy Spirit. God works in and through the human agent who cooperates with Him by choosing to help to compose the Lord's building. A holy tabernacle is built up of those who receive Christ as their personal Saviour. Of them John writes: "As many as received Him, to them gave He power to become the sons of God, even to them that believe on His name; which were born, not of blood, nor of the will of the flesh, nor of the will of man, but of God." By receiving Christ and being conformed to His will, man goes on to perfection. This building up of individual characters, which are renewed, constitutes a structure more noble than any mortal workmanship. Thus the great work of God goes forward from point to point. Those who desire a place in His church show this by their willingness to be so conformed to His will that they can be trusted with grace to impart to others. . . .
>
> To the church is given the work of making known to the world what is the fellowship of the mystery "which from all ages hath been hid in God who created all things; to the intent that now unto the principalities and the powers in the heavenly places might be made known through the church the manifold wisdom of God."[3]

In the next chapter we shall see how Christ's work in the heavenly sanctuary transforms us inwardly, making us temples fit for the habitation of God and the exhibition of His love.

---

1. Ellen G. White, *The Desire of Ages* (Nampa, Idaho: Pacific Press, 1940), 29.
2. Ibid., 165.
3. Ellen G. White, *Signs of the Times*, Feb. 14, 1900.

CHAPTER NINE

WHERE GOD'S POWER AND GLORY DWELL

Glowering at Judge Holt, chief of military justice, Edwin Stanton, U.S. secretary of war, declared, "Holt, I want you to present the charge against these deserters in the strongest possible terms."

Lips tight with concurring displeasure, Holt nodded.

Stanton continued, "We need stronger discipline in the army. The time has come when the president must yield to our wishes."

It was after the battle of Chancellorsville, a crushing defeat for the North. Several Union soldiers who had failed to march with their regiments were arrested, tried at court-martial, and condemned to death. All that was needed to carry out the sentence was President Lincoln's signature. And Stanton had chosen his prosecutor well. Judge Holt had few equals as a lawyer and forensic orator.

A few months before his death in 1894 the retired Judge Holt related: "In presenting these cases in obedience to the wishes of the secretary of war, I used all the legal acumen at my command. One morning, with my papers all ready, I proceeded to the White House; and, as I entered his private office, the president looked up with his long, sad face, saying, 'Ah! Holt, what have you there?' "

"I have some important papers for your consideration, Mr. President, with documentary evidence sufficient to condemn every man."

Lincoln looked over the papers carefully, stopping from time to time to reflect. As he read, his face grew sadder and more serious. Holding the papers in his hand for a while, he gazed pensively across the Potomac. Then, rising from his chair, he placed the folded papers in a compartment. Facing the judge, Lincoln said in sad and measured tones, "Holt, you acknowledge that those men have a previous record for bravery. It's not the first time they have faced danger, and they shall not be shot for this one offense."

Knowing that Stanton would explode with rage over the president's pardon, Holt passionately pled for the necessity of executing these men to preserve army discipline.

Rising from his chair, Lincoln riveted his eyes on the judge and asked, "Holt, were you ever in battle?"

"No, I have never been."

"Did Stanton ever march in the first line to be shot at by the enemy as those men did?"

"I think not, Mr. President."

"I tried it in the Black Hawk War, and one time grew awful weak in the knees when I heard the bullets whistle around me and saw the enemy in front of me. How my legs carried me forward I cannot tell, for I thought every minute that I would sink to the ground. The men against whom these charges are made were probably *not able* to march into battle. Who knows that they *were* able? I am opposed to having soldiers shot for not facing danger when it is not known that their legs would carry them into danger."

Then Lincoln returned to his desk, penned a few lines, handed the paper to Judge Holt, and stated with finality, "Send this dispatch ordering the soldiers' release." That day they were freed to return to their ranks.[1]

During the whole of Christ's earthly sojourn He bore our infirmities as one with us. Fully touched with the feeling of our infirmities; He was tempted in all points as we are, yet without sin. With strong crying and tears He fervently interceded for us and pled with His

Father for strength to carry out His mission to overthrow the kingdom of darkness and set Satan's captives free. Pioneer of our restoration, Trailblazer to victory, Achiever of our redemption, Bearer of our unbearable burden, Christ was the perfect Substitute for our complete failure. "In all things He had to be made like His brethren, that He might be a merciful and faithful High Priest in things pertaining to God, to make propitiation for the sins of the people. For in that He Himself has suffered being tempted, He is able to aid those who are tempted" (Heb. 2:17, 18). "God permitted His Son . . . to meet life's peril in common with every human soul, to fight the battle as every child of humanity must fight it, at the risk of failure and eternal loss."[2]

From the outset, Satan strove to undermine Jesus' decision to save us. Christ's anguish in Gethsemane epitomized His intense struggle against Satan's buffeting malice. But Christ resolved to emancipate us from slavery to sin and rebellion whatever the cost to Himself. He adopted human nature in its weakened state and relied for strength and support solely on His Father (see Rom. 1:3; 8:3; Gal. 4:4, 5; Phil. 2:5-11; Heb. 2:16, 17).[3] Achieving victory through His total submission to the Father and in His spotless innocence suffering the penalty for our sins, He became our Advocate.

Jesus' death on the cross guaranteed His right to plead the merits of His sacrifice on our behalf, as our Substitute. He doesn't intercede for us so that we can indulge in sin. Rather, His intercession provides the opportunity and grace we need for repentance, pardon, and the power to overcome sin. It was to bring to completion this work of deliverance and regeneration that He began His service as our High Priest in the heavenly sanctuary immediately after ascending to His Father. On Calvary He made full and complete provision for our salvation. In heaven, He makes full application of that provision to every willing heart.

Prophetically envisioning Christ's ascension, David sang, "When He ascended on high, He led captivity captive and gave gifts to men" (Eph. 4:8; cp. Ps. 68:18). The rich outpouring of the Holy Spirit at Pentecost signaled His inauguration as our High Priest in the heavenly sanctuary. "He gave gifts unto men, yea to the rebellious also."

What was the effect? The full and unfettered proclamation of the gospel, at the heart of which was the exaltation of Christ's sacrifice and righteousness. And what was the response? The sweeping, radical repentance of several thousand listeners, including many who had clamored for Christ's death only weeks before.

It is this work of vital character transformation that Christ has been performing ever since He sat down at His Father's right hand to make intercession for us. From this vantage point in heaven, He dispenses all the blessings of redeeming grace through the Holy Spirit. He labors not only for the responsive and obedient, but also to attract sinful, rebellious, uncaring people to the glory of His kingdom. It is His special delight to make loyal subjects of former rebels through the captivating power of the gospel. Christ has no animosity toward His enemies, only perfect love.

Just one day before Lincoln's assassination, he held a meeting with his cabinet to discuss post-war reconstruction. Some of his advisors suggested punishing the Confederacy. In response, Lincoln lifted his large hands and said, "Hold. We must extinguish our resentments if we expect harmony and union. I cannot sympathize with these feelings of revenge." This is the love-principle on which Christ and all heaven operate, though there it functions on an infinitely greater scale than we could ever envision. God has not appointed us to wrath, but to obtain salvation by our Lord Jesus Christ (see 1 Thess. 5:9). He bears no resentment or animosity toward His enemies, only perfect love exercised with infinite wisdom and mercy to secure our salvation.

On Calvary, Christ suffered for our sins—"the just for the unjust, that He might bring us to God" (1 Pet. 3:18). In mercy unfathomable, He allowed Himself to be delivered up for our offenses and was raised for our justification (see Rom. 4:25). And beyond the Cross He ever lives to make intercession for us. He sends forth a rich, magnetic stream of reconciling grace to lead us to repentance through the limitless attractions of the gospel. "As long as there is hope, until they resist the Holy Spirit to their eternal ruin, men are guarded by heavenly intelligences."[4]

What does the Father do for those who are drawn by Christ's cords of love and the power of His cross? "No sooner does the child of God approach the mercy seat than he becomes the client of the great Advocate. At his first utterance of penitence and appeal for pardon Christ espouses his case and makes it His own, presenting the supplication before the Father as His own request."[5]

Five bleeding wounds He bears
Received on Calvary;
They pour effectual prayers,
They strongly plead for me:
Forgive him, O forgive, they cry
Nor let that ransomed sinner die. —*Charles Wesley*

"As Christ intercedes in our behalf, the Father lays open all the treasures of His grace for our appropriation, to be enjoyed and to be communicated to others"[6] And even when we sin after coming to Christ, He continues to be our Advocate with the Father—because as a merciful and faithful High Priest He sympathizes with our weaknesses and seeks to work in us to will and to do of His good pleasure. "The Lord will no more cast off the humblest, lowliest believer in Jesus than he will demolish his throne. We are accepted in the Beloved."[7] As we draw nearer and still nearer to Him in daily repentance and communion, He teaches us to trust ourselves less and Him more, until we abandon self-sufficiency and make Him our whole reliance for wisdom, righteousness, sanctification, and redemption (see 1 Cor. 1:30).

Fully engaged in our soul's highest interests, Christ pleads the merits of His blood on our behalf. As we appropriate its saving power, we are recreated after His spiritual likeness. Our restoration to favor and union with God and the eradication of evil are the focus of His work in heaven's sanctuary. "Therefore He is also able to save to the uttermost those who come to God through Him, since He always lives to make intercession for them" (Heb. 7:25). We cannot initiate any part of this process; we can only respond. Through the direct influence of the Holy Spirit on our hearts, we are led to repentance and a longing for Christ and His righteousness. Christ perpetuates the power and appeal of His sacrifice by His mediation in the sanctuary above, thus immortalizing Calvary.

A literal sanctuary

The heavenly sanctuary is a literal place, vast and magnificent beyond conception and dedicated to applying divine justice and mercy to resolve the moral crisis Lucifer had instigated. In vision John saw Jesus ministering to the churches, whose interests He carefully guards and nurtures through His heavenly ministry (Rev. 1:12-20; cp. 11:19; 15:5). That ministry moves the mainspring of human affairs and the inmost workings of all surrendered lives (see Ezek. 10; Ps. 51:6, 7).

The earthly tabernacle and its services were a mere type of the glorious work that Christ is performing for us in the sanctuary above. "Christ has not entered the holy places made with hands, which are copies of the true; but into heaven itself, now to appear in the presence of God for us" (Heb. 9:24).

> The subject of the sanctuary . . . should be clearly understood by the people of God. All need a knowledge for themselves of the position and work of their great High Priest. . . .
>
> The intercession of Christ in man's behalf in the sanctuary above is as essential to the plan of salvation as was His death upon the cross. By His death He began that work which after His resurrection He ascended to complete in heaven. We must by faith enter within the veil, "whither the forerunner is for us entered." Heb. 6:20. There the light from the cross of Calvary is reflected. There we may gain a clearer insight into the mysteries of redemption. The salvation of man is accomplished at an infinite expense to heaven; the sacrifice made is equal to the broadest demands of the broken law of God. Jesus has opened the way to the Father's throne, and through His mediation the sincere desire of all who come to Him in faith may be presented before God.

> "He that covereth his sins shall not prosper: but whoso confesseth and forsaketh them shall have mercy." Prov. 28:13. If those who hide and excuse their faults could see how Satan exults over them, how he taunts Christ and holy angels with their course, they would make haste to confess their sins and to put them away. Through defects in the character, Satan works to gain control of the whole mind, and he knows that if these defects are cherished, he will succeed. Therefore he is constantly seeking to deceive the followers of Christ with his fatal sophistry that it is impossible for them to overcome. But Jesus pleads in their behalf His wounded hands, His bruised body; and He declares to all who would follow Him, "My grace is sufficient for thee." 2 Cor. 12:9. . . . Let none, then, regard their defects as incurable. God will give faith and grace to overcome them.[8]

Christ's great overcoming power is offered us through the comprehensive blessings of the new covenant, which forgives and blots out our sins, implants in us a new nature that lives in rich, enlightened accord with the requirements of God's law, and gives us unlimited personal access to God through the power of the Holy Spirit (see Heb. 8:10-12; Ezek. 36:25-29). Christ mercifully receives our prayers through His own merits and constantly applies His power to put away sin by the sacrifice He accomplished on Calvary (see Heb. 9:26).

In the daily ministration of the earthly sanctuary, God required morning and evening sacrifices to represent the perpetual availability of His saving grace through the promised Messiah's willing death on the cross. In the yearly Day of Atonement, He presented in prophetic type the final putting away of sin, a work that includes a process of judgment, the investigative phase of which He prophesied to start in 1844 (see Dan. 8:13, 14; 9:24-27).[9]

During this second phase of Christ's ministry, judgment accompanied with mediation, He invites us with heightened appeal to put away our sins and receive the fullness of His truth and grace, that He might be plainly revealed to the world through His remnant people (see Rev. 12:17; 14:1-12; 18:1-5). He wants our lives to be saturated with Calvary consciousness and Calvary love so that we can not only proclaim the everlasting gospel in its fullness but also communicate it in burning letters of gold as His living epistles. Thus the whole world will be enlightened with God's glory (see Isa. 60:1-5; 62:1-3; Zech. 10:1). It is from the sanctuary that God will sound His last appeal to the world in an exquisite symphony of love through the orchestrated efforts of Divinity, angels, and His converted people.

Those who conclusively reject the overtures of divine mercy and grace will be judged by the truth that God has revealed to them in all its heart-melting, soul-illuminating beauty (see Ps. 96:13; Rom.10:21). Since they would not put away sin through the power and sure mercies of the gospel, they must perish with their sins. This is the most painful and agonizing outcome of the judgment; it is a work that God reserves with anguished reluctance to the end of the contest between good and evil. In the meanwhile, the danger is not that God will harden His heart and prematurely terminate our probation, but that we will perniciously harden our hearts against His truth and grace, scorning His mercy as a thing of little account (see Ps. 95:6-9; Acts 7:51-60).

Soon Christ's sanctuary work will end, not in futility, frustration, or vexation, but in righteousness. When the deacon Stephen voiced his final appeal to the Israelites to accept the true Messiah, his listeners rushed forward to kill him for his unwelcome testimony. As they closed in on him with murderous rage, Stephen saw Christ standing at the right hand of the Father to signal approval of His martyr's fearless witness for truth (see Acts 7:54, 55). Christ's standing up at that moment to encourage Stephen discloses the depth of His loving regard for His faithful martyrs and the intensity of His interest in their ambassadorial mission as citizens of His kingdom.

When Christ concludes His work of mediation and judgment in the heavenly sanctuary, He will again stand up for the children of His people. This time He will come to rescue them from the powers of evil devoted to their extermination because they held high the banner of truth amid the world's scorn (see Dan. 12:1; Ps. 60:2-5, 12). He and His "celestial cavalry" will gallop forth at lightning speed to rescue, vindicate, and glorify His ransomed church, which keeps the commandments of God and has the faith of Jesus. Then, taking them to His kingdom, He will introduce them to the endless glories and untold wonders of His love as they inquire in His temple to behold the beauty of the Lord, whose light and truth led them there even before their translation. With joy ineffable they shall praise Him in His tabernacle forever and ever.[10]

Shall we not with racing desire and swift steps rise to meet Him who is so soon to come? "Draw me, we will run after thee: the king hath brought me into his chambers: we will be glad and rejoice in thee, we will remember thy love more than wine: the upright love thee" (Song of Sol. 1:4, KJV).

---

1. This historical account is adapted from J. E. Gallagher, *Best Lincoln Stories Tersely Told* (Chicago: M. A. Donahue and Co., 1898), 89-92.
2. Ellen G. White, *The Desire of Ages* (Nampa, Idaho: Pacific Press, 1940), 49.
3. Some richly illuminating references from the Spirit of Prophecy regarding Christ's human nature, which He assumed that we might receive adoption as His children, are: *The Desire of Ages*, 49, 117; *Selected Messages* (Hagerstown, Md.: Review and Herald, 1958), 1:252- 256. See also 2 Cor. 5:17-21; 1 Pet. 2:21-25.
4. White, *Signs of the Times*, June 6, 1895.
5. White, *God's Amazing Grace* (Hagerstown, Md.: Review and Herald, 1973), p. 68.
6. Ibid.
7. White, *Signs of the Times*, June 6, 1895.
8. White, *The Faith I Live By* (Hagerstown, Md.: Review and Herald, 1958), 203.
9. White, *The Great Controversy* (Nampa, Idaho: Pacific Press, 1950), 489.
10. See also *The Great Controversy*, 491.
11. See Rev. 19:7-13; Eph. 2:6-8; Pss. 27:45, 46; 43:3, 4; Rev. 20:4.

CHAPTER TEN

SOMEDAY HE'LL MAKE IT PLAIN

David could not help noticing the pattern. "Why is virtue so often married to misfortune," he wondered, "and evil to prosperity?" "Behold," he wailed, "these are the ungodly, who are always at ease; they increase in riches. Surely I have cleansed my heart in vain, and washed my hands in innocence. For all day long I have been plagued, and chastened every morning" (Ps. 73:12-14; cp. Job 21).

One would not expect complaints like this to be in the Bible, but they are, and no one stated them so boldly as Israel's royal psalmist.[1] Life's injustice seems to make godly living appear—sometimes, at least —like a frustrating mockery. Built into the very fibers of our being is the sense that justice must ultimately be served, that evil will not triumph over good, nor shall error nullify truth. If there is no final reckoning, no vindication of right and vengeance upon iniquity, no ending of evil and eternalizing of righteousness, then the universe is indeed marooned in moral futility and presents before us an impassive procession of scintillating stars on a voyage into nothingness, a dazzling, frozen symmetry exquisitely calibrated to mindless order, a resplendent amphigory that negates all meaning.

But God's Word projects no such blindly mechanistic view of the cosmos. Rather it certifies with ringing assurance, "Ascribe greatness to our God. He is the Rock, His work is perfect; for all His ways are justice, a God of truth and without injustice; righteous and upright is He" (Deut. 32:3, 4). "Righteousness and judgment are the habitation of his throne" (Ps. 97:2, KJV). "He has prepared His throne for judgment. He shall judge the world in righteousness, and He shall administer judgment for the peoples in righteousness. . . . The Lord is known by the judgment He executes" (Ps. 9:7, 8, 16; see also Eph. 1:7-14; 3:8-12).

Scripture presents God's judgment and judgments as central to the security of the universe and the health of His relations with all created beings. His judgment is squarely based on His clear and exact definition of all that He requires of us. That is why, in Hebrew, Scripture uses the same word—*mishpat*—for judgment (as a process) and judgments (as laws and decrees). God administers justice for the sake of punishing the wicked and vindicating the righteous. His moral nature is integral to His identity and proceedings, and it is unalterable. Further, His application of justice is always in perfect accord with the requirements of His law explicitly defined in His Word.

The preceding may seem like a dry, academic statement. But considering the rarity of impartial justice on earth, the revelation of God's gracious and attentive fairness is heartening. How many people (especially among the poor and oppressed) have known justice delayed, denied, distorted, or inequitably applied! With all too disturbing accuracy Isaiah stated the problem: "Justice is turned back, and righteousness stands afar off; for truth is fallen in the street, and equity cannot enter. So truth fails, and he who departs from evil makes himself a prey" (Isa. 59:14, 15).

God's love will not allow such injustice to go forever uncorrected. By means of the gospel He brings the universe into a state of unshakable moral equilibrium and order (see Pss. 146:5-10; 147:2-6). "He hath made with me an everlasting covenant, ordered in all things, and sure" (2 Sam. 23:5, KJV). With infinite love, wisdom, mercy, and justice He will rectify all wrongs and vindicate all that is true and right. In the judgment, this purpose will be triumphantly consummated to the full satisfaction of all honest-hearted inquirers throughout the universe.

Ironically, however, this alienated world looks with glaring disgust at the concept of a divinely appointed judgment. Out of the depths of its moral disorder, it defiantly asks, "Where is the god of judgment?"—as though the idea that God would judge anyone were absurd in the highest degree! (see Mal. 2:17). Solomon declared, "An ungodly witness scorneth judgment" (Prov. 19:28, KJV). But human contempt and demonic malice do not deter God from carrying out His purposes. Without equivocation or apology, God's Word declares: " 'He has appointed a day on which He will judge the world in righteousness' " (Acts 17:31). "He cometh to judge the earth: he shall judge the world with righteousness, and the people with his truth" (Ps. 96:13, KJV).

It is this certainty that inspired Paul to reason with his hearers concerning "righteousness, self-control, and the judgment *to come"* (Acts 24:25, italics supplied). The implication here is that the judgment is a future event. In Revelation 14:7, we find that God's last gospel appeal to the world proclaims the beginning of the investigative phase of His judgment: " 'Fear God and give glory to Him, for the hour of His judgment has come.' "

A set time for judgment

God permits time for the issues to reach a crisis point. This is the primary reason He reserves the convening of His judgment to the time of the end, when the great controversy between good and evil has run its course and exhibited the full scope of its inner workings. He declares, "When I choose the proper time, I will judge uprightly" (Ps. 75:2; cp. Isa. 46:8-12; Hab. 3:2, 3; 2 Pet. 2:1-9). He certainly knows best how to time this crucial event and pace its proceedings. Haste or needless delay in carrying out this vital work would be fatal to its success. "For every matter there is a time and judgment" (Eccles. 8:6).

From the Protestant Reformation onward, diligent students of God's Word recognized that the hour of God's judgment was approaching. This dawning enlightenment accords with God's promise to reserve till " 'the time of the end' " the unveiling of prophetic mysteries that pertain to the last days (see Dan. 12:4-13; 11:35; 8:26, 27). Consecrated servants of God who cleanse their characters in the blood of the Lamb and the Word of God discern "both time and judgment" (Eccles. 8:5; cp. Dan. 12:11; Rev. 7:13, 14).

From the late 1790s on, students of prophecy saw with increasing clarity and mounting conviction that the prophetic period of 2,300 days identified in Daniel 8:13, 14 as the appointed time for God's sanctuary to be cleansed was destined to climax in 1843 or 1844.[2] In late 1844, Advent believers discovered that this terminal date marked the time for the final Day of Atonement, during which God judicially reviews the moral state of the world. These believers saw that majestic scene prophetically unveiled in Daniel 7:

> The thrones were cast down [i.e., set in place], and the Ancient of days did sit, whose garment was white as snow, and the hair of his head like the pure wool. . . . The judgment was set, and the books were opened (Dan. 7:9, 10, KJV; cp. Mal. 3:1-5).

We can see from this passage that one of the cardinal objectives of the judgment is to establish Christ's right to reign as the Supreme Sovereign of the universe. In a manner of speaking, He places His government and character on moral audit before the universe that He might be justified in His sayings and overcome when He is judged (Rom. 3:4; cp. Ezek. 21:25-27).

God settles the issues

People accuse God of failing to intervene for the sake of justice. Infected with the spirit of the great accuser, they charge God with being arbitrary, negligent, and unreasonable. But Isaiah 5:3, 4, 16 explains that God does everything possible to restore even the most damaged souls to spiritual wholeness and that when this work does not succeed, it is because the objects of His grace deliberately refuse to be regenerated. God vindicates His character by fully disclosing His actions and invisible, though powerful, influences on each heart. With universal reach, He upholds the right and redresses the wrong definitively, unerringly conclusively.

It is essential to recognize the spirit in which God conducts His work of judgment. He does not carry out this ministration as a cold, detached jurist, but with longing desire to save our souls and to demonstrate the accessibility of His redemption for all. He is not willing that any should perish but that all should come to repentance and a saving knowledge of the truth.

Israel's high priest wore a breastplate containing 12 precious stones bearing the names of the 12 tribes of Israel. Scripture calls this priestly accouterment "the breastplate of judgment" (see Exod. 28:15-30), signifying that our Redeemer's work of judgment is carried out mercifully and is vitally fused with His mediatorial grace. While the judgment is in progress, Christ continues to woo the wandering hearts of humankind with intensified appeal (see Joel 2:28-32; Matt. 24:14). Extending mercy and the opportunity to repent, He offers to bestow on us a new heart capable of living in joyous, enlightened harmony with His law.

In the gospel, mercy and truth are met together, righteousness and peace kiss each other. But those who exploit or reject God's offered mercy must ultimately reap what they have chosen to sow (see Gal. 6:7, 8; Rom. 11:22). God's mercy is not an invitation for us to trifle with His justice or dally with evil, but to receive pardon, salvation, and restoration to His moral image. Its purpose is to reconcile and restore our souls, which have been alienated by sin from the life of God.

James, the brother of the Lord, wrote, "Mercy triumphs over judgment" (James 2:13). This does not mean that mercy negates judgment or renders it obsolete. Rather, it indicates that through having borne the penalty for our sins, Jesus opened a universally accessible fountain of pardon and redeeming grace for every willing recipient. All who accept this offer are spared from coming into condemnation in the judgment. How merciful a release and how royal an act of restoration to divine favor! It magnifies God's throne as the habitation of justice and judgment, an impregnable fortress of truth, upheld by mercy (see Ps. 89:14; Prov. 20:28, KJV).

Because of the destiny-deciding effects of the judgment, Christ warns us not to regard it with indifference (see Matt. 22:1-13; 25:1-13; Luke 21:34-36). An ungodly witness scorns judgment (see Prov. 19:28).[3]

God's judgments are a great deep, incomprehensible to natural human wisdom (Ps. 36:6; cp. Rom. 11:33–12:2). It's not the proud and self-sufficient, but the meek whom God will guide in judgment and show His way—that, by means of His grace, they might order their lives aright before His throne. Those who are casual about their accountability to God today will be desperately concerned about it after their probation closes (Rev. 6:14-17). However, those who take God's judgment seriously now and accept His salvation will not despair in the ultimate hour of confrontation with their destiny. They do not come into condemnation in the judgment (see John 5:24; 1 John 4:17, 18).

By virtue of His sacrifice for us and full adoption of our nature, Christ is our Judge (John 5:23-29). His angels, ministering spirits sent forth for our salvation, are His witnesses (Rev. 4, 5). Satan is the plaintiff and accuser (Zech. 3). God's professed people are the defendants and chief exhibits of His grace.

God judges His people

Some evangelical Christians have expressed strong opposition to the teaching that God's people will be judged. They insist that this teaching casts a shadow of doubt across the security of the redeemed. But this contention misses the beautiful assurance of the gospel. God wishes to show what His grace has accomplished in enabling His people to abide in Him and keep His commandments in highly adverse circumstances (Rev. 12:17; 14:12). The Word plainly declares: "The Lord will judge His people" and "judgment must begin at the house of God" and "we must all appear before the judgment seat of Christ" (Heb. 10:30; 1 Pet. 4:17, KJV; 2 Cor. 5:10). Satan accuses God's people day and night before the universe. In the judgment,

God vindicates them and demonstrates that while the devil's charges are true with regard to the saints' record of sin, the power of the gospel has made the saints perfectly whole in moral nature. God's people, then, are exhibit A in proving the efficacy of the plan of salvation (Job 1; Prov. 27:11).

Some time ago an atheist challenged a certain Pastor Hughes, a Methodist minister, to a debate on the validity of the gospel as a life-changing force. Hughes's response reveals the reason for the judgment and why it will weigh the life record of God's people by the same standard and with the same thoroughness brought to bear on the lives of the lost. In reply to the atheist's challenge Hughes said:

> As conventional debates usually lead to nothing, let us have one on new lines. I will gather a hundred men and women to assemble on the platform in the debate hall. They shall witness of the saving work of Christ in their lives. You can cross-examine them as much as you like. But you, on your part, are to bring a hundred men and women who have been redeemed from their sinful lives by your atheistic philosophy.

Needless to say, the debate was never held. Sinners saved are the gospel's best evidence.

On what standard is the judgment based? God's law as illuminated in the life and teachings of Christ defines the whole duty of humankind (see Eccles. 12:13, 14; 1 Pet. 2:21; cp. James 2:12). Our words, actions, and motives constitute our character and form the influence of our lives. All these are taken into explicit account in the judgment. Compassionately, God considers our opportunities to come to the light of His truth (see Ps. 87). He has all the contents and context of our lives unerringly recorded in His books of record and remembrance (Dan. 7:10; Rev. 20:12, 13).

In discussing the subject of divine judgment with a young assistant attorney general from the state of Michigan, I asked him, "Besides his having a clear mastery of the law, what qualities would you hope to find in an ideal judge?" Reflecting on this for a few moments, he replied, "Compassion, understanding, impartiality, the ability to weigh extenuating circumstances while not blurring issues of justice, and the need to uphold the law." It is just such qualities as these that Jesus, our heavenly Judge, possesses in infinite measure. In the judgment He discloses His untiring but oft-unnoticed deeds of love, His persevering efforts to woo, win, and seal all hearts to Himself (see Pss. 40:4-14; 48:9-11; 139:17, 18). It is this context of unfathomable grace and ineffable love that suffuses the judgment with a golden light of glory and inspires the irrepressible praise of the onlooking universe.

God's judgment magnifies the gospel

God wishes to retain the name of every human being in the Lamb's book of life. He does so for all who embrace His offer and submit to His loving authority and saving grace. How He rejoices to blot out the record of our sins! How it grieves Him to have to blot anyone's name from the book of life because of sins retained and rebellion cherished (see Exod. 32:32; Acts 3:19; Rev. 3:5).

The thought of the judgment is not meant to make believers either self-righteous or morbidly apprehensive. Properly considered, it will accentuate our need for grace, for no flesh shall be justified in God's sight (see Pss. 130:1-4). It is through Christ's merits alone, credited and appropriated, that we are saved from sin. So, the judgment, instead of eclipsing the gospel, magnifies it by highlighting the infinite grace of God to redeem our souls from eternal ruin. It explicitly demonstrates the gains of Calvary.

Regarding the judgment, our individual responsibility is to search our own hearts and refrain from judging others (see Matt. 7:1-5; Rom. 14:7-13; 2 Cor. 13:5; cp. Pss. 139:23, 24; 19:9-13). "We would all be more slow to judge, if we realized that the judgment we utter transfers us instantly from the judge's bench to the prisoner's bar."[4]

In the judgment as represented in the Hebrew sanctuary service, the people were called upon to search their hearts while meditating on the saving merits and intercession of the divine Substitute (see Lev. 16:23, 29, 30; cp. Ps. 51). In this service, the blood was sprinkled profusely on the mercy seat, thereby signifying Christ's ministry of intercession for us—which He performs jointly with the work of judgment. It is our privilege and duty to confess our sins now so that they can be blotted from our lives and from the books of record in heaven (1 Tim. 5:24). This work is the cleansing of the sanctuary spoken of in Daniel 8:13, 14 (cp. Heb. 9:23).

Ironically, while the judgment proceeds in the courts above, earth's inhabitants are feverishly mounting new heights of blasphemous disregard for God's law and government (see Rev. 11:18, 19). They rage against the light and defy the moral law of the universe at the very time their lives are under judicial examination (see Mal. 3:1-5, 13-18).

Judgment's final result

What will be the final, enduring result of the judgment? The full vindication of God's character through a complete resolution of all issues that require an explanation. The judgment will reveal that God draws an eternal distinction between good and evil, truth and error. Myriads of innocent people have suffered great loss, including life itself, because they have been condemned in secular or ecclesiastical courts for upholding the causes and principles that God commends. In the end, however, they will come forth holy, harmless, undefiled—fully vindicated and highly honored for their fidelity to truths that earthly courts and councils have despised. Thus, many who are now first shall be last, and the last shall be first.

The judgment will guarantee God's right and responsibility to eradicate all sin from the universe eternally (see Nah. 1:9; Rev. 16:5-7; 19:1, 2; 1 Cor. 15:24-28).

> In the day of final judgment, every lost soul will understand the nature of his own rejection of truth. The cross will be presented, and its real bearing will be seen by every mind that has been blinded by transgression. Before the vision of Calvary with its mysterious Victim, sinners will stand condemned. Every lying excuse will be swept away. Human apostasy will appear in its heinous character. Men will see what

> their choice has been. Every question of truth and error in the long-standing controversy will then have been made plain. In the judgment of the universe, God will stand clear of blame for the existence or continuance of evil. It will be demonstrated that the divine decrees are not accessory to sin. There was no defect in God's government, no cause for disaffection. When the thoughts of all hearts shall be revealed, both the loyal and the rebellious will unite in declaring, "Just and true are Thy ways, Thou King of saints. Who shall not fear Thee, O Lord, and glorify Thy name? . . . for Thy judgments are made manifest." Rev. 15:3, 4.[5]

Thus shall the presence and power of sin eternally end. Sin and impenitent sinners will be eradicated. Then justice will roll down like waters and righteousness like a mighty stream (see Amos 5:24). Never again will spiritual disease assail the universe. Every being will overflow with joyous praise for God, full confidence in Him, and reverent submission to His all-gracious will. This glorious resolution is the outflow of God's self-revelation through the judgment. "Zion hears and is glad, and the daughters of Judah rejoice, because of Your judgments, O Lord" (Ps. 97:8; cp. 48:11). In this auspicious setting, with all strife and discord ended, our all-glorious King shall reign in righteousness, and God shall be all in all to the eternal joy and satisfaction of the entire universe (see 1 Cor. 15:28).

---

1. Many commentators attribute Psalm 73 to the priest Asaph. Its superscription may be read either "A psalm *of* Asaph" or "A psalm *for* Asaph." Ellen White credits David with authorship of this psalm. It is certainly Davidic in structure and tone. See *Seventh-day Adventist Bible Commentary*, vol. 3:1149.

2. For a clear and detailed exposition of the prophetically decreed timing and nature of the judgment, which commenced October 22, 1844, read "The Investigative Judgment" in Ellen G. White, *The Great Controversy* (Nampa, Idaho: Pacific Press, 1950), 479-491.

3. A dream Ellen White had sets forth impressively its solemn issues; see "The Judgment," *Testimonies for the Church* (Nampa, Idaho: Pacific Press, 1948), 4:384-387. This chapter is well worth reading.

4. Maltbie D. Babcock, *Thoughts For Every-Day Living* (New York: Scribner's, 1901), 4.

5. White, *The Desire of Ages* (Nampa, Idaho: Pacific Press, 1940), 58.

CHAPTER ELEVEN

THE REMNANT—AS A DEW FROM THE LORD

Seventy years of captivity had gone by for the nation of Judah. Homecoming days had arrived. How thrilling the thought of returning to their native land far westward! Thrilling for some, that is. Many of the Jews had been born in captivity. Persia, not Palestine, was their native land. They preferred to tarry in the land of captivity where life was pleasant, prosperous, and secure. They lacked a clear sense of their commission to reveal God's virtues in the midst of a sin-darkened world. They forgot their calling to shine from the vantage ground of their own city and nation as God's light to the world (see Isa. 62:1-3).

Out of the hundreds of thousands or perhaps millions who could have returned to Judah to repopulate their homeland and resume their special work for God, only fifty thousand chose to make the journey. The rest were content to stay behind, loving the present world and preserving memories of their religion as a nostalgic but fading heritage rather than an imperishable, life-giving trust.

But even the remnant who returned to Judah did not arrive in the perfection of righteousness. Once in Judah, they quickly backslid and contracted marriages with people from neighboring heathen tribes. Ezra 9:6-15 records Ezra's prayer of confession and intercession for this group who were rapidly departing from their distinctiveness as God's representative people. Fortunately, they did amend their ways under Ezra's strong leadership (see Ezra 10). Herein lies the ultimate distinction between the true remnant and the nominally religious. The remnant repent of their sins and forsake them, but worldly religionists justify themselves in their disobedience to God's will and Word. They devise a changeable standard to suit their own inclinations and convenience.

Identity of the remnant

What characteristics mark God's remnant? They adhere faithfully to His eternal law and testimony (see Revelation 12:17). When we compare the latter text with Revelation 19:10, we discover that they also have the guiding light of the spirit of prophecy. God's last-day people are those who willingly serve as agents through whom He makes "restoration of all things, which God has spoken by the mouth of all His holy prophets since the world began" (Acts 3:21). They are the final generation in an unbroken line of light-bearers whose supreme desire is to glorify God and rightly represent His truth to the world. " 'As for Me,' says the Lord, 'this is my covenant with them: My Spirit who is upon you, and My words which I have put in your mouth, shall not depart from your mouth, nor from the mouth of your descendants, nor from the mouth of your descendants' descendants,' says the Lord, 'from this time and forevermore.' " (Isa. 59:21).

Heaven is the land of the remnant's spiritual nativity. They have not seen it yet, except by faith through the promises of God's Word. They are animated by a heavenly hope, which will be abundantly rewarded in due course. "They desire a better, that is, a heavenly country." Having their citizenship in heaven, they live in harmony with its ways. By their conversation and conduct they confess that they are pilgrims and strangers on earth and are eagerly looking for the coming of their Savior. "Therefore God is not ashamed to be called their God, for He has prepared a city for them" (Heb. 11:13-16; cp. Phil. 3:20).

The remnant have a special bond of closeness to Christ, formed through their humble, loving attachment to Him. "The Lord is near to those who have a broken heart, and saves such as have a contrite spirit" (Ps. 34:18). Those who regard themselves as spiritually better than others are oblivious to their own sinfulness and pride. They do not know the Lord, even though they may be actively engaged in religious service and produce impressive results (see Matt. 7:21-23). "Self-exaltation must be renounced by those who profess to love God and keep His commandments, or they need not expect to be blessed by His divine favor."[1] Jesus stated, " 'Everyone who exalts himself will be humbled, and he who humbles himself will be exalted' " (Luke 18:14; cp. 1 Pet. 5:5-7). Christ washed the feet of His proud disciples. He did so to teach us that true greatness is exhibited in the spirit of humble, loving service and that we must never allow ourselves to feel superior to the lowliest of God's children. It is no wonder, then, that foot-washing is one of the apostolic practices that is restored to the remnant church of the latter days.

The true remnant honestly regard themselves as less than the least of all saints and fervently prize the truth that they are not saved by works of righteousness but according to God's mercy, by the washing of regeneration and the renewing of the Holy Spirit, which He sheds abundantly upon all who receive Christ as Savior. It is no wonder then that Paul wrote of the "remnant according to the election of *grace*" (Rom. 11:5, italics added)—not according to self-avowed preeminence in spiritual attainment.

Message and mission of the remnant

> Today the remnant people of God are to glorify His name by proclaiming the last message of warning, the last invitation to the marriage supper of the Lamb. The only way in which they can fulfill God's expectations is by being representatives of the truth for this time.[2]

We see then that God's remnant not only have a message to proclaim, but a character to exhibit through the practical application of the message they bear. They are to be living epistles whose gospel message is easy to read and appeals to everyone open to the spirit of truth.

Through the remnant God makes His wisdom stand out in contrast to the heresies and delusions of the last days (see Matt. 24:24; 2 Thess. 2:9-12; cp. Joel 2:32). It is essential, therefore, for the remnant to have a healthy spiritual experience as well as a firm grasp of sound doctrine. To those who receive it, the gospel imparts power, love, and a sound mind. Humanity's restoration to the image of God is the essential purpose of the gospel. Never does truth drive us into fanaticism and harshness of word or action. Rather, the truth as it is in Jesus makes us Christlike.

Christlikeness of character combined with purity of teaching is the twofold secret of the remnant's influence. Truth alone can correctly represent God and sanctify the human heart (see John 8:31-36; 17:17). But the theory of truth detached from Christ and His imparted life is a dry husk.

> Theology is valueless unless it is saturated with the love of Christ. True Christianity diffuses love through the whole being. It touches every vital part—the brain, the heart, the helping hands, the feet—enabling men to stand firmly where God requires them to stand, lest the lame be turned out of the way. The burning, consuming love of Christ for perishing souls is the life of the whole system of Christianity.[3]

God's remnant have a special commission. It is the final proclamation of the gospel as embodied in the threefold message of Revelation 14:6-12. This message calls everyone to worship the Creator with uncompromising purity and belief in His Word. It comes in the latter days, when truth is largely obscured through tradition, science falsely so-called, and doctrines of demons posing as advanced revelation. Unavoidably, then, heaven's final message has strong elements of warning and denunciation to clear the way for every honest person to approach God without impediment or diversion from the path of life.

God's people have been divinely commissioned to call the faithful out of Babylon. This call is not to be given in a caustic spirit of condemnation, but with compassionate appeal. After all, in God's eyes Babylon is "a prison for every foul spirit, and a cage for every unclean and hated bird" (Rev. 18:2). But many in its communion, though honest and sincere, may have difficulty discerning Satan's underhanded work. Yet, because they recognize the disparity between the teachings of Scripture and the creeds of their church, they are uneasy. People in this predicament must be compassionately led into the light of present truth and not treated as heretics and rebels.

God's true sheep will in due course joyfully leave Babylon in response to the true Shepherd's voice. How important then that we weave the characteristics of Christ into our own presentation of truth. If we do not faithfully echo the voice and manner of the Shepherd who laid down His life for the sheep, we shall in a sense be false witnesses, bearing the correct theory of the truth, perhaps, but misrepresenting its essential character. Yet, however compassionately and considerately the remnant bear heaven's message, it will provoke massive resistance from those who remain entrenched in apostasy—especially from the religious leaders who want to hold on to the prestige and wealth that comes of their connection with Babylon.

Trials of the remnant

In vision, Zechariah, prophet to the remnant of Jews who returned from captivity, saw the condition of God's people exemplified by Joshua the high priest (see Zech. 3). Joshua stands before the Angel of the Lord pleading for God's mercy on behalf of His afflicted people. Satan strides boldly forward to resist him, alleging that Israel's sins disqualify them from God's favor.

Joshua doesn't deny Satan's charges. He stands before the Angel not to defend God's people but to confess their sins, typified by the filthy garments he wore into the tabernacle. He can only point to their repentance, humiliation, and trust in the sin-pardoning mercies of the Redeemer.

Zechariah caught the vision of the gospel appropriated and applied. This vision is reflected in J. H. Stockton's great hymn:

Come every soul by sin oppressed,
There's mercy with the Lord,
And He will surely give you rest
By trusting in His word.
For Jesus shed His precious blood
Rich blessings to bestow;
Plunge now into the crimson flood
That washes white as snow.
Only trust Him, only trust Him, only trust Him now;
He will save you, He will save you, He will save you now.

In response to Joshua's repentance and complete trust in the merits of a promised Savior, he was given a change of raiment—signifying the bestowal of Christ and His righteousness. This is the universal antidote to sin.

> Zechariah's vision of Joshua and the Angel applies with peculiar force to the experience of God's people in the closing scenes of the great day of atonement. The remnant church will then be brought into great trial and distress. Those who keep the commandments of God and the faith of Jesus will feel the ire of the dragon and his hosts. Satan numbers the world as his subjects; he has gained control even of many professing Christians. But here is a little company who are resisting his supremacy. If he could blot them from the earth, his triumph would be complete. As he influenced the heathen nations to destroy Israel, so in the near future he will stir up the wicked powers of earth to destroy the people of God. Men will be required to render obedience to human edicts in violation of the divine law.
>
> Those who are true to God will be menaced, denounced, proscribed. They will be "betrayed both by parents, and brethren, and kinsfolks, and friends," even unto death. Luke 21:16. Their only hope is in the mercy of God; their only defense will be prayer. As Joshua pleaded before the Angel, so the

remnant church, with brokenness of heart and unfaltering faith, will plead for pardon and deliverance through Jesus, their Advocate. They are fully conscious of the sinfulness of their lives, they see their weakness and unworthiness; and they are ready to despair.

The tempter stands by to accuse them, as he stood by to resist Joshua. He points to their filthy garments, their defective characters. He presents their weakness and folly, their sins of ingratitude, their unlikeness to Christ, which has dishonored their Redeemer. He endeavors to affright them with the thought that their case is hopeless, that the stain of their defilement will never be washed away. He hopes so to destroy their faith that they will yield to his temptations, and turn from their allegiance to God. . . .

But while the followers of Christ have sinned, they have not given themselves up to be controlled by the satanic agencies. They have repented of their sins and have sought the Lord in humility and contrition, and the divine Advocate pleads in their behalf. . . .

Nothing in this world is so dear to the heart of God as His church. It is not His will that worldly policy shall corrupt her record. He does not leave His people to be overcome by Satan's temptations. . . .

As the people of God afflict their souls before Him, pleading for purity of heart, the command is given, "Take away the filthy garments," and the encouraging words are spoken, "Behold, I have caused thine iniquity to pass from thee, and I will clothe thee with change of raiment." Zechariah 3:4. The spotless robe of Christ's righteousness is placed upon the tried, tempted, faithful children of God. *The despised remnant are clothed in glorious apparel, nevermore to be defiled by the corruptions of the world. . . .*

While Satan has been urging his accusations, holy angels, unseen, have been passing to and fro, placing upon the faithful ones the seal of the living God. . . . "These are they which follow the Lamb whithersoever He goeth. These were redeemed from among men, being the first fruits unto God and to the Lamb. And in their mouth was found no guile: for they are without fault before the throne of God." Revelation 14:4, 5.[4]

The above selection from *Prophets and Kings* highlights several important facts about the remnant:

- Satan and his followers will bring God's last-day remnant into great trial and distress.
- This opposition comes because they are resisting Satan's supremacy and submitting to God's power.
- While the remnant is sorely under siege, their greatest concern is not protection from their enemies, but to be right with God through repentance of sin and submission to His work of grace.
- The remnant are keenly aware of their past failures and of their present weakness and unworthiness.
- Satan tries to rob them of their courage and fill them with a sense of condemnation and despair.
- But the remnant have truly repented of their sins and have not given themselves up to Satan's control.
- Christ defends His people and purifies them through this time of fiery trial before probation's close.
- Out of weakness the remnant are made strong. They have nothing to say in their own praise or defense, but put all their faith and hope in the merits of Christ's saving sacrifice.
- Christ perfects His work in the remnant and seals His people to Himself.

God's remnant people are keenly aware of their need for the atoning blood of Christ—particularly in these last days. Freely availing themselves of its power, they are described as washing their robes of character to make them white in the blood of the Lamb (Rev. 7:13, 14). This work of deep inward transformation gives credibility and irresistible momentum to their work for the Lord despite the staggering trials they face. Floods of spiritual power will be poured out upon the remnant to give impetus to the final proclamation of the gospel. Christ is exalted in the fullness of His glory and honest souls who have been deceived by Satan's deceptions are then liberated to worship Him in spirit and in truth (see Rev. 18:1-5; Isa. 60:1-5). "And the remnant of Jacob shall be in the midst of many peoples, like dew from the Lord, like showers on the grass, that tarry for no man nor wait for the sons of men" (Mic. 5:7; cp. Ps. 68:1-13).

Triumph of the remnant

The conflict between truth and error, the loyal and the apostate, will be fierce, but not fruitless. Many will joyfully depart from Babylon and gratefully embrace the gospel in its unalloyed truth and beauty (see Isa. 48:20, 21).

> It shall come to pass that whosoever shall call on the name of the Lord shall be delivered: for in mount Zion and in Jerusalem [God's last-day church] shall be deliverance, as the Lord hath said, and in the remnant whom the Lord shall call (Joel 2:32, KJV; cp. Jer. 23:3, 4).

Others, presently in the visible remnant but not growing in grace and the knowledge of Christ as their Lord and Savior, will merge with the ranks of Babylon, where their sympathies and values lie. These facts were strikingly presented to Ellen White in vision:

> I saw two armies in terrible conflict. One army was led by banners bearing the world's insignia; the other was led by the bloodstained banner of Prince Immanuel. Standard after standard was left to trail in the dust as company after company from the Lord's army joined the foe and tribe after tribe from the ranks of the enemy united with the commandment-keeping people of God. . . .
>
> The battle raged. Victory alternated from side to side. Now the soldiers of the cross gave way, "as when a standard bearer

> fainteth." Isaiah 10:18. But their apparent retreat was but to gain a more advantageous position. Shouts of joy were heard. A song of praise to God went up, and angel voices united in the song, as Christ's soldiers planted His banner on the walls of fortresses till then held by the enemy. The Captain of our salvation was ordering the battle and sending support to His soldiers. His power was mightily displayed, encouraging them to press the battle to the gates. He taught them terrible things in righteousness as He led them on step by step, conquering and to conquer.
>
> At last the victory was gained. The army following the banner with the inscription, "The commandments of God, and the faith of Jesus," was gloriously triumphant.[5]

Triumphant, transformed, and glorified, the remnant will be able to declare with the apostle Paul, "I am not ashamed, for I know whom I have believed and am persuaded that He is able to keep what I have committed to Him until that Day" (2 Tim. 1:12).

The remnant are God's faithful people who love Him and therefore obey Him. In the last days they are the depositories of God's fully restored gospel free of all distortions. At Satan's instigation the whole world will seek to destroy God's remnant people through religious persecution conducted by church and state united. But under the anointing of God's Spirit, this embattled group of believers will arise to proclaim the everlasting gospel with purity, power, courage, and love. When they do so, many in the enemy's camp will separate from Babylon to join the faithful, thus becoming part of the remnant, which keeps the commandments of God and has the faith and testimony of Jesus. Together they will be glorified and rescued when Jesus comes.

---

1. Ellen G. White, *Testimonies for the Church* (Nampa, Idaho: Pacific Press, 1948), 4:221.
2. Ibid., 8:153.
3. White, *Signs of the Times*, May 10, 1910.
4. White, *Prophets and Kings* (Nampa, Idaho: Pacific Press, 1943), 587-591.
5. *Testimonies*, 8:41.

CHAPTER TWELVE

THE GUIDING LIGHT OF PROPHECY

Pastor Mead was astounded to hear a colleague say, "I don't see why our church places so much emphasis on prophecy. I think it's a distraction from the gospel and a digression from the great charter of Matthew 28:19, 20."

After recovering from his initial shock, Pastor Mead asked the other minister, "Have you considered that Matthew 28:19, 20 is itself a key passage of prophecy? Here Jesus indicates that His gospel is to be preached in its fullness throughout time and to all nations. That's prophecy number one, and it's being progressively fulfilled. Then He promises to be with His disciples always, and He has; that's prophecy number two. Finally, He declares that He will be with them to the *end of the world,* a clear and definite prophecy that the world in its present state will end. Truly, my friend, the gospel and prophecy are inseparably joined. They do not conflict with each other."

Pastor Mead's reply is forcible in its logic. The gospel first came to the world in the form of a prophecy (Gen. 3:15), and the entire Hebrew system of worship from *aleph* to *taw* was a symbolic prophecy of the gospel (see Isa. 53; Heb. 8–10). Jesus said, " 'This gospel of the kingdom will be preached in all the world as a witness to all the nations, and then the end will come' " (Matt. 24:14). What believer can fail to recognize how quickly this prophecy is being fulfilled in our generation? To omit or diminish Christ's assurance regarding His return and His prophecies of preceding events (Matt. 24; Mark 13; Luke 21) would be to preach a truncated gospel. His second coming consummates His redeeming work for humanity and is therefore integral to the gospel.

The focal point of all eschatology (i.e., prophecy about the last days), is Christ's second coming, which involves the final conquest of all evil and the visible establishment of His kingdom. Prophecy gives us practical instruction on how to relate to the events and issues of the past, present, and future, while holding Christ in clear, steady, ever-brightening view. Peter points out that the prophetic word is as a light shining in a dark place until the day dawns and the day star arises in our hearts (see 2 Pet. 1:19, KJV). Christ is that day star, otherwise called the Bright and Morning Star (see Rev. 22:16).

Regarding the dramatic events crowding the Passion Week, Christ told His disciples, " 'I have told you before it comes, that when it does come to pass, you may believe' " (John 14:29). And concerning His betrayal by Judas (an event entirely unforeseen by the disciples), Jesus stated, " 'I tell you before it comes, that when it does come to pass, you may believe that I am He' " (John 13:19). Christ gave us prophecy to help establish our faith in Him.

Christ also gave it to protect us from the insidious delusions Satan has formulated to nullify truth and justify rebellion. Using confused and egocentric religious teachers, Satan offers his own twisted interpretations of prophecy—interpretations that employ the words and symbols of Scripture, but do not "rightly divide the word of truth" nor harmonize with God's law and testimony (see Matt. 24:11, 24; Isa. 8:20; 2 Pet. 3:1-3). That is why it is essential to interpret prophecy by the Bible rather than to impose our own concepts on it (see 2 Pet. 1:20, 21).

So, we need to be judicious in our study of prophecy—but we should not refuse to investigate this major branch of Bible teaching.

Prophecy is a gift of the Spirit and has a prominent part in guiding us from the wilderness of this world to Paradise restored. In the plainest words possible, Scripture declares, "Do not quench the Spirit. Do not despise prophecies. Test all things; hold fast what is good" (1 Thess. 5:19-21). We cannot remind ourselves too often that we must "test all things" by the Scriptures.

As an additional aid to our understanding of present truth's relationship with eternal truth, God has given His remnant church the guiding light of the Spirit of Prophecy. He has bestowed this gift on His church, not to replace or revise the Scriptures, but to magnify them and emphasize those portions that have a special bearing on our time.[1]

A panoramic outline of events

Jesus gave a panoramic outline of events that will usher in His second advent (see Matt. 24; Mark 13; Luke 21). He pointed to the prophecies of Daniel as especially vital for obtaining our bearings in the last days (Matt. 24:15). In Revelation the Lord pronounces a special blessing on those who read and hear and keep the things that are written in His prophetic Word, for the time is at hand (see Rev. 1:3). Moreover, Revelation 10 in conjunction with Daniel 12 brings to view a great gospel movement at the time of the end, consisting of people who explain the prophecies (including the coded time elements) of Daniel and Revelation and who exemplify the instruction contained in these prophetic books. Their heaven-sent, Spirit-propelled message draws in adherents from every race, nationality, and language. Thus, the united witness of all truth-loving people swells into a crescendo of appeal (the "loud cry") that calls all of God's people to leave Babylon and to take their stand with the advocates of truth (Rev. 18:1-5).

Prophecy exalts the truth and exposes error. It charts the history of God's providences to advance His cause and to end Satan's power to deceive and destroy. This entire controversy unfolds in the ambiance of God's irrevocable determination to give everyone inalienable freedom to choose a spiritual master—Christ or Satan. Bible prophecy is always linked with spiritual lessons designed to attract us to Christ and the power of His unchanging gospel. No wonder Satan is so opposed to the guiding light of this gift and labors to keep our minds distracted lest we obtain our spiritual bearings from God's prophetic Word.

> As we near the close of this world's history, the prophecies relating to the last days especially demand our study. The last book of the New Testament Scriptures is full of truth that we need to understand. Satan has blinded the minds of many, so that they have been glad of any excuse for not making the Revelation their study.[2]
>
> Ministers should present the sure word of prophecy as the foundation of the faith of Seventh-day Adventists. The prophecies of Daniel and Revelation should be carefully studied, and in connection with them the words, "Behold the Lamb of God, which taketh away the sins of the world." The twenty fourth chapter of Matthew is presented to me again and again as something that should be brought to the attention of all. We are living in the time when the predictions of this chapter are fulfilling. Let our ministers and teachers explain these prophecies to those whom they instruct.[3]
>
> The light of prophecy still burns for the guidance of souls, saying, "This is the way, walk ye in it." It shines on the pathway of the just to commend and on the unjust to lead to repentance and conversion. Through its agency sin will be rebuked and iniquity unmasked. It is progressive in the performance of its duty to reflect light on the past, the present, and the future.[4]

The world's steady moral decline, the increase in violence, the globalization of apostasy through union of church and state, spirits of demons working miracles to open the way for nearly universal acceptance of advanced delusions, a coalition of world religions, a fanatically driven Sunday law, persecution of God's commandment-keeping people by angry religionists, false christs, false prophets, the rise of the ultimate antichrist, futile peace talks, war, famine, pestilence, global financial crisis, burgeoning natural disasters and human-made catastrophes, the latter rain versus false revivals, the seven last plagues, Christ's glorious return and the resurrection of the righteous, the overthrow of Satan's kingdom, the glorification of God's people—these are the major premillennial elements of prophecy with which many are familiar. Many books masterfully explain this whole panorama of events. Yet there remains a keystone feature of prophecy that sometimes receives too little attention—the great *character lessons* enfolded in the prophetic visions. To miss these lessons is ultimately to miss the whole purpose, the interior significance, of prophecy. After all, what lasting gain is ours if we master the charts of coming events but our personal lives are not charted by the Master? Paul declared, "Though I have the gift of prophecy, and understand all mysteries and all knowledge, and though I have all faith, so that I could remove mountains, but have not love, I am nothing" (1 Cor. 13:2).

Plainly, the mere knowledge of sound doctrine—including a grasp of coming events—does not result in salvation. We must also be sanctified by the truth and imbued with divine love. It is love for Christ and His appearing that constitutes one a true Adventist.

Why Christ waits

Knowing that the last days would be clogged and crowded with distractions, delusions, and difficulties, Jesus warned believers not to grow lax over the seeming delay of His return, not to drift back into worldly ways and imply by action or attitude that our Lord is dilatory in His movements (Matt. 24:48; Luke 21:34-36). Christ patiently tarries for the sake of humanity's salvation, not because His plans have lost clarity or momentum. He tells us that we may hasten the day of His return by fervently laboring to advance the spread of the gospel worldwide (2 Pet. 3:12).

Christ's message to Laodicea and His parable about the ten virgins are designed to arouse us from spiritual lethargy and self-satisfaction. They clearly point to the danger of our becoming apathetic instead of increasingly fervent as time hurtles toward eternity.

The only effectual remedy to our spiritually fog-bound condition is to draw constantly closer to Christ in fellowship and service. We will then clearly recognize that His "delay" in returning represents a mercifully extended opportunity for the human race to be saved through the gospel. Grasping this point, we will employ these additional probationary hours to grow in grace and usefulness of service to our Savior. All who exemplify in their lives the fruit of prophetic guidance become a savor of life unto life to those who welcome the voice of the Master speaking through His earthly witnesses. In response, God's faithful people come out of Babylon with joy and singing. They respond to the invitation and appeal of God's message and do not feel condemned, judged, or despised by the messengers. How different is the spirit of God's true witnesses from the spirit of those who promulgate the mark of the beast while disregarding all reasonable refutation of Babylon's fallacies.

Despite all opposition, God's messengers are imbued with the spirit of their Master. Only thus can their words and actions reveal the deep and morally sound purpose of the Bible's last and most intense warning to a spiritually bewildered society caught in the convulsive throes of earth's final movements.

> Those who are wise shall shine like the brightness of the firmament, and those who turn many to righteousness like the stars for ever and ever. But you, Daniel, shut up the words, and seal the book until the time of the end; many shall run to and fro, and knowledge shall increase.
>
> Many shall be purified , made white, and refined, but the wicked shall do wickedly; and none of the wicked shall understand, but the wise shall understand (Dan. 12:3, 4, 10).
>
> Who are these arrayed in white robes? . . . These are the ones who came out of the great tribulation, and washed their robes and made them white in the blood of the Lamb (Rev. 7:13, 14).

Throughout the pages of Daniel and Revelation—and, indeed, of all Bible prophecy—Christ the Lamb of God shines forth with a stellar brightness that banishes the deepest satanic darkness and the dullest of human feelings.

> When the books of Daniel and Revelation are better understood, believers will have an entirely different religious experience. They will be given such glimpses of the open gates of heaven that heart and mind will be impressed with the character that all must develop in order to realize the blessedness which is to be the reward of the pure in heart.
>
> The Lord will bless all who will seek humbly and meekly to understand that which is revealed in the Revelation. This book contains so much that is large with immortality and full of glory that all who read and search it earnestly receive the blessing to those "that hear the words of this prophecy, and keep those things which are written therein."[5]

That light still shines

The bright beams of the light of prophecy cannot be put out, no matter how hard God's many enemies strive to extinguish them. John Fulton, missionary to Fiji, tells the story of an evangelistic meeting he held in the courthouse in the town of Nanukoloa in the early 1900s. He came at the invitation of Ratu Joni, the district chief, who was so impressed by *The Great Controversy* that he invited Fulton to preach on the subjects contained in the book.

Just prior to that engagement, a violent storm had destroyed the local Protestant church. The chief had given its minister permission to conduct services at the courthouse while the church was being rebuilt. The minister had hung a large lamp from the ceiling and set out various furnishings for the services of his church. When he learned that Fulton was using the courthouse to preach the Advent message, the minister became so incensed that he strode into the meeting in his ecclesiastical gown and interrupted Fulton's sermon.

"Do you wish to say something?" Fulton asked in a friendly manner.

"Yes I do," the minister retorted. "That's our church's light."

Not wishing to engage in controversy, Fulton replied, "I am sorry if our using it displeases you. Do what you think is best."

Reaching up, the minister extinguished the lamp and stalked out of the meeting. Several in the audience then lit their small lanterns and set them on the table by which Fulton was preaching. Just then, Chief Ratu Joni entered and sat down near the door. Noticing that the large ceiling lamp was unlit, Joni whispered to the man next to him, "What's the matter with the big lamp?"

"The Protestant minister came and put it out," he replied.

"He did?" asked Ratu Joni, astonished and indignant. Dashing off, he found the minister and shouted, "You ought to be ashamed of yourself. Do you think you can put out the Adventist light by an act like this? The Adventist light comes from the Bible, and you can never put it out. Look up and see the mountains around you, where the towns are many. You will see, the Adventists will go to all those places and set up their light, and the cause of error and all who cleave to it shall lose much."[6]

When these words were spoken a century ago, the world church had fewer than 88,000 members. Today, it has over 12 million members, and the ranks are steadily, inexorably swelling with those who love truth more than popularity and the delusive comfort of tradition.

The lamp of prophecy is inextinguishable. Those who walk in its ever-brightening rays are indeed an illuminated people—burning and shining lights who, under heaven's blessing, point the world to the Lamb of God so soon to come and overthrow Satan's dominion and sweep God's ransomed, restored people through the star-vaulted heavens into His kingdom, with all its rapturous wonders and endless joys.

> For Zion's sake I will not hold My peace, and for Jerusalem's sake I will not rest, until her righteousness goes forth as brightness, and her salvation as a lamp that burns. The Gentiles shall see your righteousness, and all kings your glory. You shall be called by a new name, which the mouth of

the Lord will name. You shall also be a crown of glory in the hand of the Lord, and a royal diadem in the hand of your God (Isa. 62:1-3; cp. 60:1-5).

Lift up the trumpet, and loud let it ring: Jesus is coming again!
Cheer up, ye pilgrims, be joyful and sing; Jesus is coming again!
Echo it, hilltops; proclaim it, ye plains: Jesus is coming again!
Coming in glory, the Lamb that was slain; Jesus is coming again!
Coming again, coming again, Jesus is coming again!
—Jessie E. Strout

---

1. See Rev. 12:17; 19:10; 22:9. For a masterful article on the role of the Spirit of Prophecy in God's last-day movement, see Uriah Smith's "Introduction" to Ellen G. White, *Patriarchs and Prophets* (Nampa, Idaho: Pacific Press, 1958). Just as informative and perspicuous is R. F. Cottrell's "Introduction" to Ellen G. White's *Spiritual Gifts*, vol. 1, which you can find on pages 133-143 of her *Early Writings* (Hagerstown, Md.: Review and Herald, 1945).

2. White, *Christ's Object Lessons* (Hagerstown, Md.: Review and Herald, 1941), 133.

3. White, *Gospel Workers* (Hagerstown, Md.: Review and Herald, 1948), 148.

4. White, *My Life Today* (Hagerstown, Md.: Review and Herald, 1952), 42.

5. White, *Testimonies to Ministers and Gospel Workers* (Nampa, Idaho: Pacific Press, 1967), 114.

6. See Eric B. Hare, *Fulton's Footprints in Fiji* (Nampa, Idaho: Pacific Press, 1985), 159-161.

CHAPTER THIRTEEN

WE SHALL BEHOLD HIM!

Never was there a more forlorn gathering. The apostles stood and gazed intently at the receding form of their King as He ascended heavenward. Long after He faded from view, they continued peering in the direction of His departure. Unutterably silent, motionless, sad. Then their lonely, dejected thoughts were dispelled by the sound of a voice, exceptionally kind, yet tinged with mild reproof. They turned to see two men standing by them "in white apparel, who also said, 'Men of Galilee, why do you stand gazing up into heaven? This same Jesus, who was taken up from you into heaven, will so come in like manner as you saw Him go into heaven' " (Acts 1:10, 11).

This reminder echoes Christ's promise to His disciples only six weeks earlier:

> "Let not your heart be troubled; you believe in God, believe also in Me. In My Father's house are many mansions; if it were not so, I would have told you. I go to prepare a place for you. And if I go and prepare a place for you, I will come

again and receive you to Myself, that where I am; there you may be also" (John 14:1-3).

Christ's return is a certainty that His messengers have anticipated from the beginning of earthly time. At Solomon's portico shortly after Pentecost, Peter declared, " 'Jesus Christ . . . was preached to you before, whom heaven must receive until the times of restoration of all things, which God has spoken by the mouth of all His holy prophets since the world began' " (Acts 3:20, 21). Christ returned to heaven to prepare a place for a people who are prepared to dwell there through accepting His sacrifice and gladly receiving His truth fully restored. For those who take the Bible seriously, Christ's second coming is not a matter of doubt, dispute, or tenuous hope but of fervent expectation (see Heb. 10:37-39).

Signs of His second coming

Christ deems it important that we understand the signs pointing to His soon coming. Most of the events He foretold regarding the last days indicate a steady decline in human morality stemming from society's progressive rejection of God's Word. Paralleling this pervasive moral declension are persecution, social disorder, financial instability, wars, family strife, and natural disasters of increasing frequency and intensity. All this turmoil directly or indirectly results from humanity's contempt for God's law (see Isa. 5:20-25; 24:4-6).

In the face of these weighty signs that collectively herald the nearness of His coming, Jesus spoke these encouraging words, " 'When these things begin to happen, look up and lift up your heads, because your redemption draws near' " (Luke 21:28). Keeping our eyes fixed on the triumphant outcome of prophetic events, we are strengthened to endure the difficulties of the way. Imbued with the spirit of Paul's buoyant optimism, those who love and serve God can confidently declare, "I consider that the sufferings of the present time are not worthy to be compared to the glory which shall be revealed in us' " (Rom. 8:18).

Jesus does not wish us to live under a cloud of anxiety concerning last-day events. At the same time, however, He warns us not to be complacent in our confidence—hence His admonition to be watchful and ready at all times and to fend off the worldly spirit of this age that threatens to engulf all civilization (see Matt. 24:36-44). Two millennia ago Christ spoke this pertinent warning to the final generation of His followers: "Because lawlessness will abound, the love of many will grow cold. But he who endures to the end shall be saved" (Matt. 24:12, 13; cp. Heb. 10:36-39).

> Everything in the world is in agitation. The signs of the times are ominous. Coming events cast their shadows before. The Spirit of God is withdrawing from the earth, and calamity follows calamity by sea and by land. There are tempests, earthquakes, fires, floods, murders of every grade. Who can read the future? Where is security? There is assurance in nothing that is human or earthly. Rapidly are men ranging themselves under the banner they have chosen. Restlessly are they waiting and watching the movements of their leaders. There are those who are waiting and watching and working for our Lord's appearing. Another class are falling into line under the generalship of the first great apostate. Few believe with heart and soul that we have a hell to shun and a heaven to win.
>
> The crisis is stealing gradually upon us. The sun shines in the heavens, passing over its usual round, and the heavens still declare the glory of God. Men are still eating and drinking, planting and building, marrying, and giving in marriage. Merchants are still buying and selling. Men are jostling one against another, contending for the highest place. Pleasure lovers are still crowding to theaters, horse races, gambling hells. The highest excitement prevails, yet probation's hour is fast closing, and every case is about to be eternally decided. Satan sees that his time is short. He has set all his agencies at work that men may be deceived, deluded, occupied and entranced, until the day of probation shall be ended, and the door of mercy be forever shut.

Solemnly there come to us down through the centuries the warning words of our Lord from the Mount of Olives: "Take heed to yourselves, lest at any time your hearts be overcharged with surfeiting, and drunkenness, and cares of this life, and so that day come upon you unawares." "Watch ye therefore, and pray always, that ye may be accounted worthy to escape all these things that shall come to pass, and to stand before the Son of man."[1]

An ancient king's dream

It was the golden age of ancient civilization six centuries before the birth of Christ. Nebuchadnezzar, the brilliant 25-year-old emperor of Babylon, was contemplating the destiny of his kingdom and the world. While engaged in these cogitations one night, Nebuchadnezzar fell asleep and had a dream. He awoke the next morning much troubled. He knew his dream had enormous significance, but he could not recall any of it. None of his scientists, occult priests, or magicians was able to provide him the slightest clue as to the content of the dream or what it meant. But God revealed the dream to the captive Jew Daniel, who in turn told the king his dream and its interpretation (see Daniel 2).

In amazingly succinct symbolism, Nebuchadnezzar's dream portrayed world history from his day to the end of time. We won't give a detailed exposition of it here, but will emphasize two facts about the dream: First, that it points to the establishment of God's eternal kingdom of righteousness in conjunction with the overthrow of all evil; and second, that we are on the verge of seeing these events take place.

We can easily deduce the nearness of these events from the chronological sequence presented in the dream. The first four empires—Babylon, Medo-Persia, Greece, and Rome—are long extinct. Since the dismemberment of ancient Rome, we have been living in a divided, militaristic world. Soon shall appear the "stone cut out without hands," which represents the second coming of Christ ushering in of His kingdom of glory. This event is confirmed by the closely related prophecies of Revelation, especially chapters 12 through 19.

Let us rejoice that God's sovereign shall prevail and that "the end is drawing nearer, the end for which we sigh"—an end that is really the most glorious of new beginnings (see 1 Cor. 15:24-28).

Our Lord's return signals the irreversible overthrow of Satan's rule. Just prior to that event, the devil stages a frantic effort to retain his foothold. Knowing that he cannot suppress the proclamation of Christ's second coming, Satan will try to pre-empt it by impersonating Christ (see 2 Thess. 2:4-9).[2] Due to a faulty interpretation of prophecy and their lack of sanctification, the vast majority of the human race will be taken in by the spurious second coming and will end up worshiping Satan and succumbing to the mark of the beast (Rev. 13:8).

However, none need be taken in by this deception despite Satan's spectacular displays of supernatural power, for God will not permit Satan to counterfeit the manner of Christ's second coming. Consequently, it is crucial for us to understand the manner and outcome of the true Messiah's appearing. It cannot be too deeply etched into our thinking that

> none but those who have fortified the mind with the truths of the Bible will stand through the last great conflict. To every soul will come the searching test, Shall I obey God rather than men? The decisive hour is even now at hand. Are our feet planted on the rock of God's immutable word?[3]

Part of our needed fortification is to have a clear understanding of the manner, purpose, and effects of Christ's return. If we master this information in loving devotion to the spirit of truth, then we shall not be deceived by the greatest and most cunning of Satan's miracles. Here is a quick review of the facts connected with Christ's return:

- Every person on earth will see Christ simultaneously, not just a limited number of people in different parts of the world (see Rev. 1:7).
- All the heavenly angels, numbering into the billions, will accompany Christ in the unveiled splendor of their celestial

glory (see Matt. 24:30, 31; 25:31; Luke 9:26).
• Every ear will hear Christ's voice and trumpet (see 1 Thess. 4:16; John 5:25).
• All the righteous dead will be awakened from their graves in a glorified state. The righteous living will also be glorified (see 1 Cor. 15:50-55; Phil. 3:20, 21).
• Christ will not actually stand on the earth, but will catch up all His people to meet Him above the planet and take them to His Father's kingdom (see 1 Thess. 4:16, 17).
• The surface of the earth will break up from earthquakes, volcanoes, and massive tectonic shifts that will remove mountains and islands, and this sphere will be enrobed in fire (2 Pet. 3:9-12).
• All the living wicked will be slain by the brightness of Christ's appearing. That same light shining upon the righteous will glorify them because they have walked in the light of Christ's example and Word (2 Thess. 1:7-10).

Satan cannot counterfeit any of these well-defined events.

The object of Christ's return

Jesus has decreed that prior to His return, the pure gospel will preached to the world for a witness to all nations (Matt. 24:14). Because of the thoroughness with which the world will have been instructed and entreated by those who faithfully witness for God, none will have the excuse of ignorance concerning God's moral requirements and His offer of the grace and power necessary to live in harmony with those requirements.

When Christ comes again " 'in the glory of His Father, with His angels, . . . He will reward each according to His works' " (Matt. 16:27; cp. 25:31-46). Jesus isn't teaching here that we are saved by our works, but that our works are the test of our faith, the demonstration of our response to the *work of His grace*. On this issue, multitudes are deceived by a false gospel that teaches that works have no bearing whatever on our salvation. Before coming to that blasé conclusion, such persons need to consider Colossians 1:10; 2 Thessalonians 1:11, 12; 2:16, 17; Titus 3:5-8; James 1:4, 25; 2:14-26; 3:13; and 1 Peter 1:17; 2:12. Not one passage cited here leaves the slightest impression that our works have the least saving merit. They all teach, however, that those who are truly saved will be very diligent to work in harmony with God's will that He may be honored by our consecrated service "for it is God which worketh in you both to will and to do of his good pleasure" (Phil. 2:13, KJV). This clarifies the meaning of Christ's declaration,

> "Behold, I am coming quickly, and My reward is with Me, to give everyone according to his work. I am the Alpha and the Omega, the Beginning and the End, the First and the Last. Blessed are those that do His commandments, that they may have the right to the tree of life, and may enter in through the gates into the city" (Rev. 22:12-14).

The day will finally come when our trials cease. Those who love and worship the Lord will ascend with Him to His kingdom, glorified, ennobled, happy beyond compare. "Eye has not seen, nor ear heard, nor have entered into the heart of man the things which God has prepared for those who love Him" (1 Cor. 2:9). Prophets have had glimpses of heaven's glory and have stretched the limits of human language to depict something of the boundless magnificence of that celestial kingdom (see Isa. 11:6-10; 65:17-25; Rev. 21, 22). Even so, the vastness and profusion of its glory are infinitely beyond our present grasp.

> Language is altogether too feeble to attempt a description of heaven. As the scene rises before me, I am lost in amazement. Carried away with the surpassing splendor and excellent glory, I lay down the pen, and exclaim, "Oh, what love! what wondrous love!" The most exalted language fails to describe the glory of heaven or the matchless depths of a Saviour's love.[4]

> Oh, let us contemplate the amazing sacrifice that has been made for us! Let us try to appreciate the labor and energy that heaven is expending to reclaim the lost, and bring them back to the Father's house! Motives stronger, and agencies more powerful, could never be brought into operation; the exceeding rewards for right-doing, the enjoyment of heaven, the society of the angels, the communion and love of God and His Son, the elevation and extension of all our powers throughout eternal ages—are these not mighty incentives and encouragements to urge us to give the heart's loving service to our Creator and Redeemer?[5]

Preparing for translation

In the meanwhile, as we watch and wait—wistfully, with palpitant expectations of our Lord's return, it is our privilege to

> dwell in this world in the atmosphere of heaven, imparting to earth's sorrowing and tempted ones thoughts of hope and longings for holiness; . . . coming closer and still closer into fellowship with the Unseen; like him of old who walked with God, drawing nearer and nearer the threshold of the eternal world, until the portals shall open and we shall enter there.
>
> [The one who enters there] will find himself no stranger. The voices that will greet him are the voices of the holy ones, who, unseen, were on earth his companions—voices that here he learned to distinguish and to love. He who through the word of God has lived in fellowship with heaven, will find himself at home in heaven's companionship.[6]

"Beloved, now we are the children of God; and it has not yet been revealed what we shall be, but we know that when He is revealed, we shall be like Him, for we shall see Him as He is. And everyone who has this hope in Him purifies himself, just as He is pure" (1 John 3:2, 3; cp. Col. 3:1-17).

Even now the gates of the Holy City, the New Jerusalem, swing open with welcoming luminance. Soon numberless millions will enter that gate. Shall we not make our calling and election sure in Christ that we may join that holy assemblage over whom He shall rejoice—and we with Him in responsive thanksgiving for His wondrous redeeming love?

> The city had no need of the sun or of the moon to shine upon it, for the glory of the Lamb has illumined it, and its lamp is the Lamb. And the nations shall walk by its light, and the kings of the earth shall bring their glory into it. And nothing unclean, and no one who practices abomination and lying shall ever come into it, but only those whose names are written in the Lamb's book of life (Rev. 21:23, 24, 27, NASB).
>
> "They shall walk with Me in white, for they are worthy. He who overcomes shall be clothed in white garments; and I will not blot out his name from the Book of Life, but I will confess his name before My Father, and before His angels. He who has an ear, let him hear what the Spirit says to the churches" (Rev. 3:4-6).
>
> Every creature which is in heaven and on earth . . . I heard saying: "Blessing and honor and glory and power be to Him who sits upon the throne, and to the Lamb, forever and ever!" (Rev. 5:13).

---

1. Ellen G. White, *The Desire of Ages* (Nampa, Idaho: Pacific Press, 1940), 636.
2. See also White, *The Great Controversy* (Nampa, Idaho: Pacific Press, 1950), 624.
3. Ibid., 593, 594.
4. White, *Early Writings* (Hagerstown, Md.: Review and Herald, 1945), 289.
5. White, *Steps to Christ* (Nampa, Idaho: Pacific Press, 1956), 21.
6. White, *Education* (Nampa, Idaho: Pacific Press, 1952), 127.

If you enjoyed this book, you'll enjoy these as well:

Prophets of Fire

Brian D. Jones. The author unveils the full significance of Malachi's prophecy concerning Elijah, demonstrating that God's last "Elijah" represents a movement and a people vitally engaged in God's closing work to save a spiritually lost world.

0-8163-1704-6. Paperback. US$11.99, Cdn$17.99.

Truth That Matters

Keavin Hayden. This book shares the full message of the Adventist Church in a positive and uplifting way. The author speaks regularly at churches, seminars, and camp meetings around the country. Excellent for sharing.

0-8163-1393-8. Paperback. US$8.99, Cdn$13.49.

It's Time to Stop Rehearsing What We Believe and Start Looking at What Difference It Makes

Reinder Bruinsma. In this fresh look at Adventist beliefs, the secretary of the Trans-European Division addresses what difference it makes to have doctrines. This book will captivate people who question how doctrine applies to everyday life issues.

0-8163-1401-2. Paperback. US$9.99, Cdn$14.99.

Order from your ABC by calling **1-800-765-6955**, or get online and shop our virtual store at

<www.adventistbookcenter.com>.

- Read a chapter from your favorite book
- Order online
- Sign up for email notices on new products